The Gnostic

A Journal of Gnosticism, Western Esotericism and Spirituality

Issue 1

Copyright Page and acknowledgments

The Gnostic 1, Spring 2009.

Opinions expressed are those of the contributors and not necessarily those of the publisher.

Editor: Andrew Phillip Smith

Published by Bardic Press
71 Kenilworth Park
Dublin 6W
Ireland.

ISBN: 978-1-906834-02-9

Thanks to the contributors and all others who have made this possible, including but not limited to: Tessa Finn, Alan Moore, Chris Staros, Pádraig Ó Méalóid, Dean Wilson, Miguel Conner, Lala Ashford-Brown, John Turner, Jesse Folks, Luke Valentine, Tim Freke, Eddie Campbell, John Coulthart, José Villaubia, Arthur Craddock, Will Parker, Scott Finch, Mike Grondin, Jeremy Puma, Tim Freke, Bill Darlison, Quest Books, Inner Traditions, Skylight Paths, Watkins Books.

The Gnostic

A Journal of Gnosticism, Western Esotericism and Spirituality

Issue 1

Alan Moore, John Turner, Will Parker, Jesse Folks, Scott Finch, John Coulthart, A.M. Ashford-Brown, Sven Davisson, Michael Grondin, Miguel Conner, Jeremy Puma, Luke Valentine, Dean Wilson

Edited by Andrew Phillip Smith

Bardic Press
Dublin 2009

Contents

Editorial

From the Mouth of the Demiurge

The first issue of any periodical sets the tone for the entire series. The theme of this journal (or magazine, I have little preference as to which term is used) is Gnosticism in all its forms and influences, and in all its interpretations. I would prefer to eschew definition of Gnosticism—and a glance at the contents page should illustrate well enough the scope of the journal—but some statement of aim and approach is needed. Gnosticism is the spiritual or religious system typified by the texts in the Nag Hammadi library and the sects, groups and individuals labelled as Gnostic by the heresy-hunting fathers of the Church. It can also include all movements and teachings associated with the ancient Gnostics by historical connection or by theme. Lastly, it includes modern attempts to revive Gnosticism and also modern or older spiritual teachings that may be considered akin to Gnosticism.

The Gnostic is also interested in contemporary creative people who are influenced to a greater or lesser degree by Gnosticism. On the academic side, this first issue includes an interview with John Turner, an expert on Sethian Gnosticism, a new translation of the *Gospel of Judas* and a note on translational issues in the Gospel of Thomas. Gnostic-influenced writers are featured heavily with an interview with Alan Moore, and an excerpt from a prose work inspired by William Blake, and articles on William Burroughs and Philip K. Dick. The more adventurous scholarly articles include Will Parker's examination of the magical worldview, a look at the figure of Judas outside of the New Testament, and an examination of Paul's attitude to Moses. Jeremy Puma's regular column looks at the pivotal topic of Gnosis itself. Future issues will see a continatuion of this trend, along with the exploration of related spirituality and esotericism.

The Gnostic is a 'no-budget' publication and I would like to thank the contributors and interviewees all of whom have given freely of their time. The contributors were also, without exception, punctual in their submissions and the exceedingly long development time of this first issue is due entirely to the procrastination of the editor.

Future issues will include a letters page, and readers are invited to submit letters and comments to andrew@bardic-press.com or by snail mail to the editorial address,

The Gnostic Magazine
71 Kenilworth Park
Dublin 6W
Ireland.

Andrew Phillip Smith, Dublin, 2009

Andrew Phillip Smith

An Interview with Alan Moore

Widely acknowledged to be the best and most influential writer of comics, Alan Moore is the author of many graphic novels or comic ssuch as *From Hell*, *Watchmen*, *Lost Girls*, *Promethea*, *V for Vendetta*, and *Miracleman*. Less well known but also worthy of attention are his novel *Voice of the Fire*, and his performance pieces, such as *Angel Passage*, *Snakes and Ladders* and *The Highbury Working*. His decision at the age of 40 to become a practising magician had a profound effect on his work as well as his daily life. Moore's Gnosticism is rooted in altereed state experience and the full complement of occultism and western esotericism.

Dark occult themes predominated in *From Hell*, his incisive dissection of the Jack the Ripper Whitechapel murders and late Victorian society. *Promethea* concerned a superhero figure who was a living embodiment of creative imagination, and among its highlights was an extended journey through the sephiroth of the tree of life. His multimedia performance pieces have used psychogeography as their basis, but have explored themes such as the development of identity in *The Birth Caul*, or resurrection and . Following the interview we are proud to present the first extensive printed excerpt from *Angel Passage*, his William Blake inspired piece. Alan Moore was interviewed on the telephone by Andrew Phillip Smith on January 9, 2008.

APS: What is your understanding of Gnosis?

AM: My understanding is that 'Gnosis'

means 'to know', a direct knowledge, to go and look for yourself. You don't want to be told what to believe, you don't need faith—faith is for cissies—you know because you've seen it. Magic is based upon Gnosis, and I don't really differentiate between magic and Gnosticism.

If you look back at the Gnostic religions that may have preceded Christianity—the Essenes, the mystery religions, maybe—what they relied

on was direct knowledge of the mysteries, or the ideas they were dealing with. If you look at the early disciples, the people that we are told were around Jesus, then you can't get much more Gnostic than St. Thomas, who has to stick his hand in the wound! Back then, everybody formed their own relationship to the godhead, which, as much as anything, was seen as being inside them.

Then you have the invention of Christianity, which you might view as the creation of Constantine and his lot, which was that they made this mixture of other beliefs because they needed a composite religion to solve the political problems in ancient Rome. That was invented out of a blend of other beliefs and all of a sudden they're saying it doesn't matter if you haven't had Gnosis, it doesn't even matter if we haven't had Gnosis, we've got a book, it's about these people from a long time ago, and they had Gnosis, they had divine visions, so we'll just read the book to you, no need for anyone to have Gnosis in this day and age, let's just have faith.

APS: I've been working on an introduction to Gnosticism and I was just looking at the writings of some of the heresy-hunting church fathers who accidentally preserved some of the Gnostic myths as they refuted them…

AM: Absolutely.

APS: The *Gospel of Eve* was meant to justify the practice of consuming menstrual blood and semen that was supposedly carried out in some Gnostic rituals.

AM: I've heard of that vaguely. I don't know very much about the *Gospel of Eve*. Anyway, it was meant to justify these rituals that the Gnostics were supposedly carrying out.

AM: Drinking semen and menstrual blood, these yucky things.

APS: Yes, and grinding up abortions and eating them in cakes, but the funny thing is, and the point of this, is that in the second century, orthodox Christians were accused of the same things by pagans, and of having appalling orgies.

AM: It is actually incredible when you look back at those first couple of centuries and you start to realise what a free-for-all it was. In theological terms, you've got Jesus Christ—the Christian view of Jesus Christ—as one of several competing messiahs. And you've got the Gnostics of course, like Simon Magus who of course was two different people, it was Simon the magician and Simon the Gnostic, and by conflating the two of them, it was very convenient for Christianity because they could roll it up in this neat little story of the evil travelling magician laid low literally by the power of Christ, and by conflating him with Simon the Gnostic they could also suggest that, see, this is a messiah of Gnosticism, but we were tougher. There was almost a propaganda war going on where both sides were using these tactics to undermine the credibility of the other, and there were figures like Apollonius who were seen as redeemers, and it was the Christians who won the battle—I don't think they won the philosophical battle, but the literal battle with sheer numbers. And it was a war, and when it came down to it, they were obviously not averse to slaughtering and destroying anything that got in their way.

APS: I was just rereading the beginning of *Promethea* today, and I noticed that you referred to Hypatia.

AM: Yes, well this would have been just after the time that Hypatia was skinned with clam shells by a Christian mob. Funnily enough, me and Steve Moore are currently working on *The Moon and Serpent Bumper Book of Magic*, and one of the features within it, which are spread throughout the text in the book, are called 'Old Moore's Lives of the Great Enchanters', where we're kind of going through chronologically about fifty of the people that we think are absolutely essential to magic, rather in the style of those old *Ripley's Believe it or Not*, where you have a single page feature with four or five panels, but we had to rule out Hypatia, strictly for reasons of space, but also because she was a Hermetic philosopher rather than an actual magician. We ended up going for Sosipatra?? Who is very definitely a kind of magical figure in her own right. So, we gave a passing reference to Hypatia, I think we managed to give her a walk on for one panel, because we wanted to get her in somewhere because—fucking hell, she was skinned alive with clamshells so that's got to be worth something. Sosipatra was the sort of second-century Alexandrian period female magician that we finally settled upon.

APS: And, again, in *Promethea*, the name of the modern Promethea was Sophie—a direct reference to the Gnostic Sophia?

AM: Yes, definitely.

APS: Did you ever read Morton Smith's *Jesus the Magician*?

AM: Yes, I've got that somewhere on my shelves here, but they're in terrible disarray so I'm not sure where I'd actually find it. It was an interesting book. I mean, like, my basic position on Jesus of any sort is, it all seems fine if there's not any insistence upon historicity, because that seems to be where all the major monotheistic religions become unstuck. As I understood, the original Gnostic view of Jesus—they seemed to be treating him as an idea rather than as a person, or they were interpreting what the birth of Jesus meant. They seemed to be taking it a lot less literally than the Christians of the period were. Back then, it was all a lot more flexible. Even the Christians back then certainly weren't fundamentalists in the current modern American model. They were, to a degree, flexible. I think back then they understood Bible stories as *stories*. They weren't so bluntly and brutally literal as the current

Promethea. Art J.H. Williams III © DC Comics 2008

fundamentalists, who actually haven't got much in common with the origins of Christianity at all. It goes back no further than 1930s tent-show Revivalism, I think that back then that even the Christians—I mean, they were fighting their corner and fighting it brutally—I don't think they were quite so ossified in their thinking as modern Christians with their incredibly literal attitude. The creation story for example, Christianity has been able to accept at various points in its history, different versions of the creation story, because it was understood as a story. I think that at some point there was a Jewish scholar who rewrote the creation story to make it work better with what Jews had historically found to be their situation and so it was more of a story of loss and wandering. But there were no objections because it was just a story that was revised to make it more appropriate to current circumstances. It's interesting that I was saying to my wife the other day, we were talking about the creationists and the intelligent design lobby, and we were saying, do you know how much fuss there's been within the Muslim world about Darwin's theory of evolution? And I said, absolutely none. And this is because Islam does not presume—Islam finds it ridiculous that anybody should presume—to know what was in the mind of the creator. So it regards creation myths as simply that, as stories. It doesn't really have any creation myths in the Qur'an. So they're completely relaxed about the idea of evolution or Darwinism. It's only Christianity, or Judaeo-Christianity, that seems to suffer from this because currently there are a group of people who are wilfully stupid. It's not just that they're stupid—I mean, that could be a congenital condition that wasn't their fault—but they are wilfully stupid. And they are having a disproportionate effect upon… everything in the world.

I mean, I read the science magazines and I ruefully note that the many worlds theory is back. Even though nobody likes it and even though it seems incredibly messy and convoluted and flies in the face of all common sense, and was discredited about ten or twelve worlds ago, they brought it back out of desperation because it is a solution to what they call 'the Goldilocks problem', which is that our universe is not too hot, not too cold, just right. This is a problem from the traditional scientific viewpoint because really the chances of this being a habitable universe are ridiculously tiny. So if the starting conditions had been out either way we would have had a universe where stars couldn't have formed, let alone light, so the fact that we are in such a perfect universe for us, you can see what the intelligent design lobby would make of that. So, even though, actually, perhaps it would be best just to continue to ponder this problem of why the universe is so perfect for us, what has happened is, because they're frightened of making any concessions to the ID lobby, scientists have flailed around to see if there's any theory that could sort out the mathematical problems that they're having with the odds against this being an inhabitable universe. So they've wheeled out the many worlds theory, they've now decided that—actually, they discarded it because there still wouldn't have been enough parallel universes to make the odds of this one existing that much likelier. So they've rearranged the maths so that there are now just enough universes so that one of them would be habitable. But that seems to me to be deforming actual science just as much as the creationists are trying to do. Even without people making concessions to them, they are deforming the debate. It's a thorny problem.

APS: Yes. It sounds a bit barren too. You'd hope that parallel worlds would be at least as interesting as our own world.

AM: Each of them is an uninhabitable nightmare. One of the things that did strike me as a cautious note for optimism is that, in *New Scientist* a few years ago, there was a piece by some of the people on the cutting edge of quantum cosmology, and they were saying that, according to what we now knew, in the first few micro-seconds of the universe, the term 'big bang' was made completely obsolete and irrelevant and meaningless. It just isn't complex enough to convey what we now know about the starting conditions of the universe. People were saying actually, if you want adequate terminology to talk about these things, you need to go back to Sufis, the theosophists, cabbalists and they were talking about the cabbalist and Sufi idea and theosophist idea of the universe expanding from a single point, which fits in very well with Einstein's thinking. And they were also saying that if we wanted a phrase that adequately described the primary and secondary inflation phases of the universe, then we could really do no better than Hokhmah-Binah. And there was a flurry of letters the next week, saying that this was capitulating to superstitious nonsense, but actually I can see a way in which things like Kabbalah,—basically you can use Kabbalah even if you are a complete atheist or agnostic, it still makes sense, I mean even in terms of how the universe appears out of the quantum vacuum. It still makes sense.

I could see a way in which things like Kabbalah might even reconcile this seemingly intractable debate between on the one hand the dogma of the religious fundamentalists and on the other hand, the dogma of Richard Dawkins.

APS: Yes, I was reading *The God Delusion* a few weeks ago and I was quite prepared to come out the other end of book and find myself as a rationalist atheist. Apart from having some problems with some of his arguments—he can be a bit unfair at times—basically, by the end of the book I realised that scientific, rational thinking isn't at the centre of my experience—it's just not the most important kind of experience that I have, and I'm not a scientist, so that's why

I couldn't adopt that approach.

AM: I mean, Dawkins, a lot of people like him… I liked some of his early books, but I think that a lot of scientists are getting so rattled by the creationists that they are perhaps overstating their case, in fear of being dragged back to the dark ages. But what they overlook is that, etymologically speaking, the word 'religion' shares the same root as 'ligature' and 'ligament' and I believe that it simply means 'bound together in one belief'. There's not even a spiritual connotation necessarily in there. Basically, the Conservative Party are a religion because they are 'bound together in one belief'—well, some of the time they are—and any other group you care to mention where they are 'bound together in one belief'. It's almost like a religious equivalent to the original definition of fascism, with the bundle of bound twigs. I do tend to see, in a certain sense, religion as a kind of spiritual equivalent of fascism in that I personally find it unnatural to think that we should all of us only have one root God. All of us are physically different, even identical twins, we are physically different. All of us are intellectually different, all of us are emotionally different. I find it unusual to think that we wouldn't all be spiritually different, and I think with Gnosticism as with magic, I think that it is the duty of everybody to make their own peace with the universe, in their own terms. I think that ultimately that is what all of us have to do, whether we like it or not. So that's almost like a spiritual equivalent of anarchy, which I think magic probably is. And I think that when you get people like Richard Dawkins arguing against religion they perhaps should note the religious qualities of their own thinking. You get groups like the Committee for Scientific Enquiry Into Claims of the Paranormal, with people like James Randi who seems to have devoted his life to proving that Uri Geller can't bend spoons with his mind—I mean, who cares, frankly? Evidently James Randi cared enough to, having reached the point where he could not prove that Uri Geller was not bending spoons with his mind, he made allegations that Geller was a paedophile, which is a very scientific method of approach I would have thought, and Geller successfully sued him. But people like CSICOP are following a dogma, they are claiming that anything beyond the parameter of rigorous scientific rationalism can't be true. They must all be either delusions or knowing hoaxes. This got to the point, I believe, that someone actually put to the test the claims made by astrology, and decided that people, apparently, according to astrology, people born with Mars rising should be athletic champions and there should be a high preponderance of athletic champions. So they decided that, this being, well, *then*, the twentieth century, we actually had a very high number of athletic champions, so he decided to check the records, and this guy had done pretty exhaustive research and he had found that there was a couple of percent above chance.

APS: Gauquelin, is this Michel Gauquelin?

AM: Yes, that was probably him. And he found— it was only a couple of percent above chance, but to a statistician it was enormous.

APS: And in generals, he found that Mars affect in generals too.

AM: Yes—you probably know more about this than I do. All I know about is CSICOP's response, where they had said, 'he's made a simple mistake, he's not done the maths right, and if you just look at our findings, you will find that actually there is no deviation from chance.' And then somebody who actually worked at CSICOP said, 'Well, look, I feel I have to say that you altered the evidence. Because I do believe in scientific enquiry and I feel that I have to point out that you used a smaller and smaller statistical sample, excluding, until you had got the answer you wanted.' At which point I think CSICOP fired him. So, that is cultish thinking.

APS: You know, Gauquelin committed suicide.

AM: Really?

APS: Yes.

AM: Was it after that CSICOP review?

APS: I don't know, it was in the late eighties or early nineties. [He committed suicide in

1991 and the CSICOP controversy ran from 1976 to 1982. Ed.] The psychologist Eysenck investigated Gauquelin's claims and he found that he had been extremely careful with his statistical analysis, but eventually he seems to have been ground down by it all and killed himself.

AM: Yeah, I could see how it could do that. These people at CSICOP, including some very respected people like Martin Gardner, these are people who were around when Wilhelm Reich was thrown into jail by the American authorities, basically for having funny ideas, and had all his equipment and his notes burned on the lawn of his house, and this should have outraged any scientific community that had a shred of humanity about them, or a shred of fellow feeling for another scientist, and they all were relieved that Reich was out of the picture, they never said a word about it, they never protested, in fact I think some of them even applauded the actions of the government. It doesn't really make science look very good, and my sympathies are much more with the scientists than with the creationists. But I feel like saying 'boys, boys, boys... you're both wrong.' I think this whole schism between spirituality and science—it didn't use to be that way. It's a relatively modern invention. Science is the direct blood descendant of alchemy. Yet as science has gained ground it has begun to find its parent an embarrassment, as many teenagers do, and it's tried to get it sectioned off to a home somewhere. And yet it's only because of the alchemists, only because of people like Isaac Newton or John Dee that modern science is what it is, even as far as someone like Einstein goes. There was a very nice letter in *New Scientist* after this article on how the kabbalistic view or theosophical view of the formation of the universe chimes so well with Einstein's opinions. There was a letter in from somebody who actually worked at the Museum of Theosophy which is Mme Blavatsky's former house, and was saying that Einstein's granddaughter or niece had visited the place and asked to be shown around and signed the visitor's book and had said that she had always wanted to see the place since she'd read bits of *The Secret Doctrine*, a copy of which was always open on a corner of her uncle or grandfather's desk . Which suggests that there are magical or Gnostic philosophies underlying a lot more of modern science than modern science would care to admit. I don't really think that there needs to be this vicious conflict between the spiritual and the scientific. Like I say, back at the time of the alchemists they were happy to combine all of them into the one magical science of life. And it might be that it could offer a solution to our current impasse.

APS: I feel that the postmodern culture helps this, and there's a kind of postmodern spirituality that acknowledges that whatever view of the universe you're assuming, you have your own experience, and you can't necessarily assume that the ideas you hold about the universe are objective, but...

AM: That is more or less suggesting that postmodern culture, in some ways, resembles pre-modern culture. I think that sounds pretty reasonable, and it suggests that we've come full circle. Well, not full circle, but a spiral, we're in the same place, but we're a notch higher up.

APS: One of the interesting things about the Gnostics, going back to Genesis again, is that there's no single Gnostic interpretation of Genesis. It's used as a springboard for Gnostic interpretation, but in a different way each time, the story keeps getting changed..

AM: And they're all seen as valid. Which is the exact antithesis to this view, 'No, there is one interpretation of the Qur'an, there is one interpretation of the Bible, and anything which deviates from that is blackest heresy. It's a much healthier way of approaching it, to see all of these different versions as completely valid.

APS: Did you have any religious upbringing yourself? What were your early religious or spiritual influences?

AM: Well, my earliest religious influence was a man who was in the Salvation Army. We used to call him Uncle George. I've got no idea what connection he had to my family—he certainly wasn't a relative—but I remember him bringing round little sentimental pictures of a little boy and a little girl playing...

APS: This sounds like it's going to turn into a story like Randi's Uri Geller accusations...

AM: Well, one was for me and one was for my brother, who was much prettier than I was and who Uncle George had mistaken for a girl. That was why there was the picture of a little girl playing. Religion around my house was a very strange mongrel approach to spirituality. The working class in the area where I grew up in the Boroughs in Northampton, things hadn't changed for them very much over a couple of hundred years, particularly not for the women. One of the things about industrial society is that the men went out into the future to work with the machines, and the women by and large stayed at home in the past. And things didn't change very much for them. And my grandmother, who was the matriarch dominating the house where I grew up, she had a web of superstitious beliefs...

APS: Was this the one with the birth caul?

AM: This was the one who gave birth to a son who had a birth caul. So that was one grandmother. The other grandmother was what we called around here a deathmonger, which was a phrase that I believe was used only in the Boroughs, though I stand to be corrected, they were the ones who were... because the people in the Burroughs couldn't afford proper midwives or proper funeral directors, so they had a deathmonger who would travel around and would attend to births, attend to deaths and probably attend to a lot of the stuff in between as well. I get the impression that 'deathmonger', if you'd taken it back a couple of hundred years it would probably have been wisewoman or witch.

APS: A bit like the sin-eater, you know that tradition?

AM: Yeah, something like that. Now, these were both ostensibly Christian women, my grandmother certainly who lived with us, on my mother's side, as well as superstitions she considered herself very religious. My mother would have always put Church of England on her birth certificate, although when questioned about her beliefs, it always seemed to be some sort of Buddhist belief. She believed in reincarnation.

APS: It could even be theosophy.

AM: Well, possibly. I think it was just a muddle of ideas that had been around when she was growing up. Not particularly considered, but it was just what she believed. And I don't believe that she ever saw any discrepancy between believing in reincarnation and considering herself a Christian. It was a strange idea of Christianity. Her sister, my Aunt Hilda, who was a deeply religious woman, who had a corner of her house kept for religious objects, icons and things like that. When I first became a magician and did a picture of Glycon, the second century Roman snake god, that I continue to have a rewarding relationship with. Both my Mum and my Aunt Hilda loved the picture of him at first glance, and my aunt put it up in her corner with all of this Christian stuff, which must have looked a bit strange. But, it was a very tolerant view of religion. I went to a church, it was a Baptist Church—there just happened to be a Baptist church in the area—where they had a Boys' Brigade.

APS: Yeah, the same happened to me actually. I was in a Church in Wales school but I went the Baptist chapel because of the boys' club attached to it. It was only a few years ago that I realised it was a recruitment technique for the Baptists.

AM: Yes, that's it, and they have a youth club, and opportunities to meet girls, and things like that. It wasn't so much about the religion. And indeed by that time, as I went into my teenage years, I was starting to become an atheist—I mean in the hippy ethos of the time, everyone was a de facto atheist—it would have been seen as terribly uncool to believe in God. I guess that I probably just went along with that in my teenage years. And when I'd reached the age of, I don't know, about 25, and was finally over my adolescence or whatever, I started to think about it a bit more deeply. And personally that led me to Gnostic ideas, magic and things like that, which seems to be the perfect place, that's where I feel most naturally at home.

APS: How did you pick on Glycon, or as you put it, how did he pick on you?

AM: Well, I had decided on my fortieth birthday to announce that I was going to become a magician. I should point out that I'd had a little to drink when I announced that. It doesn't make it any less heartfelt, but it explains the recklessness of announcing it more understandable. But I hadn't really got any plan. I thought I'd have to follow this through, having said it, but I haven't really got any clear idea of how to go about it. And I ended up talking to one of my oldest friends and my mentor to a certain degree and he's someone who has had, for an awful long time, since the 1970s, has had a kind of a relationship with the Greek moon goddess Selene.

APS: Yes, I read the piece about him in *London: City of Disappearances*.

AM: 'Unearthing'. Yes, that's turned out to have some peculiar ramifications as well, that are quite interesting. But I approached Steve and

I said, how do I go about this magic business, and he said, well, that a good way to start would be to choose a god, and I thought, how do I go about that, and I decided that it perhaps would just be a good thing to remain open to, and we were, I think it was during a Saturday night of recreational psilocybin abuse, that Steve suddenly said, 'Oh have you seen Alexander's serpent?' And I said, 'No, I've no idea about it, are we talking about Alexander the Great?' And he said, 'No we're talking about Alexander of Abonutichus and he had this snake god and it was really cute.' And Steve pulled out a book of Roman antiquities that had got on the cover a picture of the statue of Glycon recovered from a tomb in Tomis, which is somewhere in the Balkans, around that Black Sea area. And it was love at first sight, I just thought it was one of the strangest and yet most familiar things that I'd ever seen. This human-haired snake, I hadn't seen anything like it before, but at the same time there was this familiarity and also I felt a great kind of sympathy with the image. And I asked Steve Moore about it, and he told me this story of a kind of glorified glove puppet, the cult of which had spread as far as the emperor, Marcus Aurelius, he had gone to consult Glycon, and that the cult had survived for about 150 years after Alexander's death, which wasn't bad going...

APS: Really, it survived?

AM: And I liked the idea of this completely bogus god, because there's some interesting things about it. Alexander of Abonutichus is the first magician who we actually have hard evidence of the existence of. This is something surprised me and Steve when we were compiling our list of fifty great enchanters, but we have Gnostic gems, we have coins with images of Glycon on them, and we have the writings of Lucian, Alexander's critic where he decries the whole of the Glycon cult as this riotous fraud, which it almost certainly was. But I liked the idea of the *idea*, I liked the concept that it was the idea who was the god. It wasn't the glove puppet, the glove puppet was just something for people to focus on. Just as images in traditional religion like an image of the crucified Jesus is not actually supposed to be the crucified Jesus—although probably for the Catholics it probably is—it's like it's the idea that's important, it's not what the idea was dressed up in. So I found myself really perversely attracted to the thought that Glycon—well, Alexander was the first demonstrably provable magician, Glycon was the last created Roman god, and it's also interesting in that it shows us probably our only instance of how a god is put together—literally in Glycon's case, as Lucian describes the way in which the fake serpent's head was made. It seems to make sense. I'm not sure whether there was a speaking tube or whether Alexander was employing ventriloquism. It was one or the other. But the idea that this glove puppet conceptually could stand for the snake energy and all that that means, because the snake god is one that winds through almost every culture. Christianity obviously not excluded. And it's obvious that this is a very important symbol, and if I want to worship it under the name of Glycon in the knowledge that my god was just a second-century glove puppet, I like that. It adds an element of humility to the thing, and it's also a much safer bet than Christianity. If people were to find out that Jesus Christ was a first century glove puppet, or didn't exist, then because Christianity insists upon this sort of historicity, this historical Jesus Christ, Christianity would fall to pieces. And there would be no need for it to, because a lot of the core ideas are very good ones. But if it was ever conclusively proven that there was no Jesus Christ, that any of the story didn't happen then the whole religion would fall to bits. Whereas Glycon, as a conceptual entity, the concept of Glycon undeniably exists and has existed. It's not to get focused on the physical reality of the thing, that is why I chose Glycon as much as anything. And also because he's got really lovely hair.

APS: I had a photo of him up on the computer when you were talking then.

AM: Lovely hair, it has to be said.

APS: Don't you think that there's more power in a myth if you think that it's literally true? I think for a lot of Christians that's the case. It's a myth for them, but one that they think really happened, but the rules were different in that single case, in the first century with Jesus. I mean, many Christians wouldn't acknowledge the possibility of miracles happening these days, but they think that they really happened back then.

AM: Back then the rules were different. Well, if I wanted to I could say, 'yes, these days it would be very difficult to produce a snake with a human head that could talk Greek, but back then it was a lot easier, there were a lot more of them about,' these Greek-speaking human-headed serpents.' It's much easier to actually say that the idea that there is a serpent with a human head that can talk is flatly impossible, as is a virgin birth. Don't pin all of your philosophical and spiritual ideas upon something which makes about as much sense as the Teletubbies. Conceptually, you can conceive of absolutely anything you want, but there's absolutely no point in saying that this actually existed. Whether you're talking about King Arthur, whether you're talking about space aliens, whether you're talking about Jesus, whether you're talking about Glycon. Accept that concepts have their reality, and that reality is if anything more important than physical reality. It is a different reality to physical reality, but it is no less valid. In fact, in some instances it is probably more valid in that most of our physical reality is predicated upon our internal reality. Everything in the room surrounding us started out in somebody else's mind. The world of immaterial ideas is possibly more important than the world of physical things, because it comes first.

APS: Which takes us back to Plato again...

AM: Well, yeah, it's got similarities with Plato, and that makes sense, or at least it does to me. And if you can just understand that simple thing, that the world of the mind is real, that makes sense in terms of Plato, it also makes sense in terms of William Blake, and a lot of our great visionaries. That is the way they view reality. It's the way I view reality. I'm not saying that I'm a great visionary by the way, I'm just saying that that is the way that makes most sense to me. It seems obvious. Because of the way that science has set itself up, where science cannot demonstrate in a laboratory the existence of the mind, so mind itself is beyond the province of science, which means that science is currently trying to explain that consciousness is a kind of hallucination caused by our glands. Because it's the ghost in the machine, it's something that cannot be explained in terms of Newtonian physics. And so, there's this huge debate where an awfully large part of the scientific community would really like to explain consciousness out of existence, and would explain that we're not really conscious. There are other schools which are talking about us having a kind of transpersonal consciousness, which I've got more sympathy with, but they're never going to be able to be able to prove it in a scientific forum.

APS: Is that panpsychism?

AM: It might be. It's something that's come up in some consciousness studies. I don't know an awful lot about it, but I believe that it involves something called *qualla* space Which they define as a kind of mindscape, or a kind of energy, mind energy, that actually floods the entire universe. But I'll wait until all the papers are in on that one before I make any decisions.

APS: Well, I think that panpsychism is one way of getting round it. You just say that consciousness is something that everything has on every scale.

AM: That'd work.

APS: But then you don't have to explain anything.

AM: Well, yeah, I don't know. I think that we're being pushed towards coming up with new models of consciousness and reality and existence I think that in this century that push is probably going to get a lot more accentuated.

APS: In an interview you spoke of a Gnostic experience that you had, and I think you compared it to Philip Dick's experiences.

AM: I think that the only point of comparison was that, yes, I did have this transformative magical experience. It seems to me that I had actually encountered, along with a friend who was also present—and this was mentioned in the *Unearthing* story—but we did feel that we had encountered this energy that seemed to us to be the snake god energy. This seemed to us to be Glycon, a second-century Roman snake god. Now, Glycon originally, when Alexander was selling people on the idea of Glycon, he did this by billing Glycon as the new Asclepius, as the reincarnation of Asclepius. Now I was reading one of his expositions on *Valis*, the Valis experience, and I found myself recognising a lot of things from my own experience in it. The sense of being outside time, the sense that time was a kind of an illusion. There was the Roman element in that Glycon is a second-century Roman god, which chimed with some of the Roman elements in Dick's construction of things, and then there was a bit in one of the letters in which he said, 'I've worked out who the entity is who's trying to get in touch with me, he is called Asclepius.' And at that point I thought, well, that is a bit strange. And also there was one of the Greek philosophers who claimed that he'd been contacted by Asclepius. I've got this written down somewhere, if only I can find it.

APS: Well, Socrates' final words were that he wanted a cock to be sacrificed to Asclepius.

AM: So it seems that Asclepius is a kind of a chatty deity in many respects. That was the only really strong connection with Philip Dick, along with some other elements—the timelessness, the sense that reality was not what we saw it as.

APS: That'll let me lead into another question about unitive experience. Many of the experiences that you've described are perhaps more visionary in their emphasis, and that seems to be more of your focus. My spiritual background comes more from being present and, perhaps, unitive experience. I like the way that you address that at the top of the tree in *Promethea* when she gets there everything is white and gold and…

AM: everything is one

APS: Yes, everything is one.

AM: The top of the tree was a bit of a guess. As far as I know you can't get there. I had, at least in my own terms, managed to get to all of the other spheres. So I was writing about them from what passed for first hand experience, at least for me. Chokmah was the highest I got really, which was pretty exhilarating. What I eventually figured out was, with Chokmah you are granted the vision of God face to face, you can kind of look up and see Kether, and I think that was probably what I was doing. So it's a white and gold guess, you know, with a lot of nothingness in there. Not as quick to write as one might think, it was quite a difficult episode that one, because there was a lot of space. It was the final episode of the Kabbalah thing. You know, I enjoyed that. It was an interesting experiment. For all of us—the artists, the colourists, and I think the readers responded to it.

APS: When I was looking over that today I was surprised to see that it's already five years since you finished that. What has the reaction been in that time period, and how has your thinking changed about that subject.

AM: In the time since then, I've spent at least a couple of those years working on *Jerusalem*, my new novel, which is going to be taking up most of my time for the next couple of years as well.

APS: So there's still a few years to go until we'll see that?

AM: Yeah, I'm doing *The Bumper Book of Magic*, which is developing my formal ideas about magic by putting them down on paper with Steve's help—and it's a collaboration—but we are finally honing our thesis in what I hope will be a fun, enjoyable way. That is my traditional magical work that is going into that. *Jerusalem* is something that's a bit different. It is perhaps a visionary book. Even in its title it's referring to Blake, it's talking about the area in which I grew up in which a lot of the British Civil War came to a close, where we had an unusually high population of Ranters, Moravians, Muggletonians, Levellers, Diggers, Monarchists—all of these radical, strange puritan groups and protestant groups, dissenting groups, and we had Philip Doddridge, who completely revolutionised the Anglican Church, so that it accepted dissenting religion, and did it all from

this lousy little district in Northampton.

APS: That was all just the one district?

AM: It was all just the one district, which is about half a mile square, and there's angels that were reputed to have led pilgrims, two different angels that were reputed to have led people to the same street in the Burroughs—it was obviously really popular with angels at a certain point and we've got one of the only round churches in the country that was built to mimic Solomon's sepulchre in Jerusalem. And of course, Solomon's temple was, at least according to legend, built by demons. There's a few demons in *Jerusalem*, a few angels, there's a kind of strange working-class version of God. It's a very working-class vision of an afterlife and it's based upon my thoughts about the fourth dimension. Although it's completely mad and fluorescent, there is a credible kind of rational idea in there somewhere, and as well as all these incredible supernatural characters there's also plenty of human characters: there's my grandmother the deathmonger, there's her own first baby, which she lost after eighteen months, there's Charlie Chaplin, who did his first performance when he was seven, at the Burroughs, and who came from Lambeth, as did my paternal grandmother, who was the deathmonger—she was born in the gutters on Lambeth Walk interestingly enough, and of course Lambeth was where William Blake lived. So Charlie Chaplin, my Nan, William Blake, all from Lambeth, so there's a thread of Lambeth working its way into all this. There's stuff about John Clare, there's stuff about John Bunyan, who referred to Northampton as Mansoul, which is a name which I'm taking from Bunyan for the middle part of my book. Which concerns the adventures of my younger brother Michael. He choked on a cough sweet, a Tune, when he was about three or four. He had actually got chronic tonsillitis and his windpipe was a tiny little hole, but the doctor, no doubt under pressure, had prescribed cough sweets, which is the last thing you need, and one of these lodged in his throat. And there was no transport in the Burroughs, there were no telephones and we were a good mile or two away from the hospital, however the guy next door to us had a fruit and veg business and had an old delivery lorry, and so we took my brother, who was not breathing, into a lorry and he was driven up to a hospital which, back then—it was 1958, something like that—and even if the lorry was flying, he would have been at the very minimum five minutes without breathing. And I belief it's brain death after a couple of minutes, isn't it?

APS: I don't know, it may well be.

AM: I believe it's considered to be brain death after two or three minutes. And after five minutes, it's generally all-over death. And he was back with us by the end of the week. They dislodged the Tune, they took his tonsils out. We were just glad to have him back, so we never thought much about it. But much of the central part of this book is about what my brother was doing in the couple of minutes during which he must have been technically dead. And this expands to this savage hallucinating Enid Blyton narrative that takes up the

Sketch © Eddie Campbell 2008.

middle part of the book, which is my brother and a bunch of dead kids running around in the after life. In the fourth dimension, burrowing from time to time, trying to solve a mystery, meeting Philip Doddridge, witnessing the great fire of Northampton, bumping into Oliver Cromwell... It's a lot of fun to write. Then the final third of the novel will be trying to tie it all up into some sort of glorious polemic argument. I mean, this is a mad book to embark upon. My last calculation said that it was going to be near to 750, 000 words, more than the half a million that I'd first anticipated. I mean I'm at chapter 21 now out of 35, so another eighteen months or a couple of years and I should be getting there. It's simply an attempt to talk about everything in my life, to talk about the physical world that I came from, and the mind that I exist in to a certain degree, to talk about the politics and the spirituality and the other human aspects. I suppose, contemporary life. Even though I'm only talking about half a square mile where I grew up, I'm trying to tell a story that, you couldn't say that it could be about anywhere, but it's a story that has a kind of universality about it. So that's taking up a lot of me time at the moment. A lot of my spiritual energies are being channelled into that, which is purely personal, it's not really drawing upon the iconography of the magical lore that I've absorbed and accumulated, I'm making it up as I go along. It's a very liberating experience.

APS: A Welsh poet spoke about that square mile of childhood, how you'll never know any area again as well as you knew that square mile.

AM: And I suppose that is why—it is only a square mile but I know it very, very well, at least well enough to fill what is turning out to be a 1500 page book. I don't think that is actually possible. I'm going to have to look at putting three books together in a slip case or something.

APS: Yes, the binding would come apart.

AM: I'm hoping that technology will catch up with my vision and come up with quantum glue or something, that can hold a potentially infinite number of pages together. But I'll probably have to settle for three books in a slipcase, but it's important that they are considered as one book. It's not three books. They wouldn't stand up on their own, any of them, but I think that together they're going to be marvellous.

APS: do they fit into that tripartite structure, like a body-soul-spirit kind of thing?

AM: Well, it's not quite as neat as that. It is a three-part structure. The first part is called 'The Burroughs' and it's talking largely about things that happen in the material plane, the history of this area. One of the stories is narrated by the ghost of a rough sleeper from the 1940s and 50s, a guy called Freddie Allen who was a real person. There's one chapter narrated by his ghost. There's another chapter narrated by a coyly veiled Charlie Chaplin. There's various episodes from various ordinary and not-so-ordinary characters. That's the first third of the book. The second third of the book is called Mansoul, and like I say, that takes place all in the upper Burroughs, a kind of fourth-dimensional unfolding above the district that is kind of timeless, eternal, and where there is a gang of ghost children called the Dead Dead Gang, which is a name which came to me in a dream. Like I said, it's almost Enid Blytonesque. Even though I'm talking about some very, very grown-up things, the fact that you're writing about what are essentially children, gives it the air of a children's narrative. The third part of the book will be called 'Vernal's Inquest', and what that will be trying to do, the way I hope it will work is something like a hologram, where as far as I understand it, a hologram works by basically projecting two pictures at once so that a third image comes out as a blending of the two images. What I'm hoping to do is, in the third book, to somehow overlay the sensibilities of the second book on those of the first book. I think the third book will probably have the most of the writing that people probably most associate with me, in that it will probably be a lot more modernist than the first book. And I'm hoping

that it will all come together. I've got it all plotted, but the plot is the least of the book. It's more the philosophical and emotional tone and whether all of the ideas have been properly explored and pursued, but I think it should all come together in a couple of years.

APS: I look forward to it. Because I really liked *Voice of the Fire*.

AM: Well thank you. I mean, there are elements... there are a couple of references. I mean, it's not a sequel to *Voice of the Fire*, and I've tried to avoid too many crossovers... there are a couple of points...

APS: It would be a bit of a killer for the new book if you'd had to have read *Voice of the Fire* before *Jerusalem*...

AM: Absolutely. There's a glancing reference to shagfoals. I don't think they even say their names. It's possible that the head on a stick from chapter 7 or 8 might make an appearance. We shall see. I'm trying to avoid making any kind of cute connections. Because although a number of the stories in *Voice of the Fire* took place in the Burroughs, because at one point the Burroughs was all that there was of Northampton, it was the old town. So there's a couple of crossovers, but I hope not an annoying amount.

APS: Something else that I wanted to ask you, I heard that at one point your next prose book was going to be *A Grammar* which was rumoured to have something to do with a journey from Northampton to Cardiff. I was especially interested in that because I'm from Cardiff.

AM: It was a journey from Northampton to round about Builth Wells in Wales. It was just that we bought a ruined farm over ten years ago now, in the middle of Wales, and we found out that there was a place nearby that had got a building that was called Northampton House. It was a tiny little town, Llandovery, where one of the only big buildings was called Northampton House, and we wondered why that was. We've got a place in Northampton that is traditionally called the Welsh house, and we eventually found out that it's because, probably since the Bronze age, but certainly since Saxon times, there has been a drover's path connecting Northampton with Wales. And the two pay stations [toll houses?], the one up in Northampton was called the Welsh House, the one in Wales was called the Northampton House. I originally got an idea That followed that tract of visionary countryside, taking in people like Elgar and Shakespeare and John Dee.

APS: Would that take you through A E Housman country as well?

AM: I think it probably would. So it would be kind of charting a drift of English vision. But I was originally going to do that book as my follow-up novel to *Voice of the fire* when Faith Brooker was still the editor at Gollancz and the only reason I was working at Gollancz was because I liked Faith Brooker and got on well with her, and she asked me if I would like to write a novel and I said, 'Sure' and when she asked me if I'd like to write another one, I said, 'Sure' again, and *A Grammar* was the idea that I came up with. Then Faith was kind off brutally dismissed in some kind of in-house night of the long knives—I think that Gollancz was taken over by Cassell, and was taken over by Orion, and I didn't really feel like doing another book for them. So *A Grammar* went by the wayside. And I'd only got a few pages into it, and I wasn't really... it seemed a bit over-clever the way I was approaching it, a bit mannered, and I wasn't really settling into it for whatever reason. So I put the idea aside and worked on the ABC Comics stuff for five or six years instead. And having finished that I've got a much sharper idea of what I want to do as a novel. Who knows, in the future there's a possibility that something will ignite that story, something of the sheep path might turn up in some form or another. Whether it will ever appear as a novel, I don't know, we'll have to see.

APS: How was *Voice of the Fire* received by the literary establishment?

AM: With barely a whisper. I tend to think that to some degree... most of the people who have read it have been quite impressed by it and quite enjoyed it. There weren't many reviews. I don't know if there were any reviews... well, there were a couple, and very good ones, but I think that to some degree the fact that I am primarily known as starting out as a comic book writer disqualifies me from serious literary intention. I think that we still have a kind of Jane Austen mafia, or its latter-day equivalent tending to run the literary establishment in this country. And that's fine by me. I've got no real interest in the literary establishment if the literary establishment is represented by that which wins the Booker prize, and if the artistic establishment in this country is represented by the current crop of Brit artists, then it's all a matter of taste of course, and I'm not criticizing anybody here, but for my taste I'm not really anxious to be associated with those kinds of establishments in any case. Anyway, I've been on *The Simpsons* so that's as good as being made Pope. So I think I can shrug off any lack of attention regarding *Voice of the Fire*. I only did it because I wanted to write it. And I'm really pleased with it, and the top Shelf edition with the José Villarubia pictures looks really nice. And the same thing with *Jerusalem*. I can't imagine that many people will be even willing to pick up a 1500 page book, although maybe it will be like *A Brief History of Time*, in that everyone will want one to have on their bookshelves and nobody will actually read it. The important thing from my point of view is that I actually write it. That is, when something is written and in a published form, I'm already thinking about the next project, so it's only this part of it that I really fell engaged with the work, when I'm actually doing it.

APS: Perhaps I can run a few topics past you. I'll just offer you a word or phrase. Alchemy

AM: Alchemy, to me, was one of the central pillars of existence. As I understand alchemy, it's almost all metaphor rather than metallurgy. Yes, it certainly started out as metallurgy but then you've got all of these metaphorical associations added to the meta-craft till it became almost a kind of poetry. I think that when the alchemists talked about their language of the birds, they were talking about a very symbol-laden form of poetry. I think that alchemy being referred to as the art is making something very central to magic very explicit. I believe that alchemy is the Art and I believe that Art is alchemy. I believe that any artistic act is a magical act and I think that many of the alchemists would have agreed with me. Probably Giuseppe Monteverdi for one. As I understand it, he invented opera purely to put over alchemical ideas. To me the mysteries of alchemy—i wouldn't claim to have pondered them deeply, I suspect that as with many areas of magic or Gnosticism, they have an awful lot in common with the mysteries of artistic creativity.

APS: Jung

AM: I've got a great deal of respect for Jung. I am particularly amused that when Freud first discovered Jung he was thrilled because Jung was Swiss. Here was this brilliant young mind and he was Swiss. I believe that Freud remarked at the time, 'Thank God for Jung. Now they will not be able to call it the Jewish science any more.' And yet by the end of his association with Jung, Freud was saying, 'Dear God, do not let Jung drag my beloved science down into the black mud of occultism.' Because, actually, psychoanalysis, psychology, these are talking about the mind, and as we said earlier in the conversation, science cannot talk about the mind, so Jung I think was only acknowledging something that was true, which was that all that psychoanalysis could really was was occultism in a lab coat. Occultism with a veneer of scientific respectability. It can never be a science, because it was talking about things that could not be repeated in a laboratory. It was talking about human consciousness. All it did, largely, was replace the taxonomy of the occult with a scientific taxonomy. You don't talk about 72 goetic demons any more, but you can talk about a range of obsessions or neuroses. Actually the effect would be quite the same as the 72 goetic demons, but you wouldn't be seeing them in the same way. And I think that Jung was one of the people to suddenly acknowledge that what they were doing was simply a continuation of what the occultists and Gnostics and alchemists had been doing for centuries. If you look at most of the brilliant breakthroughs and ideas

that psychoanalysis came up with, they were commonplace in societies like the Golden Dawn and commonplace in Gnostic circles or occult circles, and so Jung deserves great credit if only in that he was one of the few people in his profession to actually acknowledge the importance of the incredible web of symbols that are present in occult literature to his developing field of practice.

APS: Dan Brown and the *Da Vinci Code*

AM: I've never read it.

APS: Well, you can read it in two hours.

AM: It's obvious what it's swiped from. I think that it reminds me very, very much of when we did *From Hell* and we did that pentacle. A bit of a wonky pentacle, but a pentacle nonetheless, that links up these key points in London. And I had loads of people coming up to me and saying, 'Is that true?' And, well, are those points there? Yes. Can you draw lines between them that will make a kind of wonky pentacle over London? Yes. Are those points what I said what they were in terms of their history and significance? Yes. But on the other hand, if you've got a small enough map and a thick enough magic marker, any three points are in a straight line. And with the concentration of historical sites in a place like London, it's very easy. Almost every street corner has got something significant.

APS: The M4 is in a straight line as well.

AM: Yes. And the thing is, with Dan Brown, you've can put together a hodge-podge of facts and half-facts, and one of the things about human beings is that we have a great faculty for actually imposing an orderly pattern on absolute chaos. It's the Rorschach blot mechanism. Or the fact that we can look at the stars, the random splattering of the stars across the sky and we can imagine that those ones look like a plough, and those ones look like a lady in a chair, you know. It's one of our great human talents, and it's sometimes useful. But, no, Dan Brown is occultism lite, isn't it, it's so that people can 'ooh' and 'ah' and think that they are in touch with some profound mystery of the ages. It's a slightly more grown-up Harry Potter yarn. It's people who feel disenchanted in our modern post-industrial age. In a quite literal sense. They don't feel that there's any enchantment in their lives, and they're desperate for it.

APS: It's much worse than Harry Potter I think.

AM: I thin it is. Although I'm not a big fan of Harry Potter, I think that Dan Brown is certainly more insidious.

APS: Have you read Philip Pullman?

AM: I haven't read Philip Pullman. I've heard various reports. People say that he's quite good. I don't get a chance to read very much these days. Now that I'm working so much on *Jerusalem*, I've got a huge pile of books building up here that I really need to read. So it's really going to be a couple of years before I even get round to it.

APS: There are some genuinely Gnostic ideas in there.

AM: Yeah, I understand that that's the case. From what I understand, it's coloured by his obvious dislike of Catholicism, which I can understand, I mean I had lots of mates who were brought up Catholic and they're all simmering cauldrons of resentment.

APS: I'm living in Ireland now...

AM: Yeah, absolutely. You're in the thick of it.

APS: Well, it's all quite diminished here now. Pullman is someone who seems to have been forced towards the Dawkins position because of the amount of antagonism he has experienced from Christians.

V for Vendetta by David Lloyd © DC Comics

AM: I can understand people getting into that state, but it doesn't help. It doesn't help to polarise because all you end up being is a mirror image of what you're opposing. You develop your own dogmas as a counterpoint to theirs. If they go over the top in attacking you, you go over the top in attacking them. Truth is not actually served by either of these activities. I prefer to stand apart from the debate. Just me and my snake.

APS: Maybe I can close by looking at Gnostic themes in a couple of your early works. I was talking to a young friend of mine who surprised me by seeing Gnostic ideas in *V for Vendetta*. Actually I think that he had only seen the film.

AM: Well, I've not seen the *V for Vendetta* film...

APS: Well, let's not get on to that.

AM: But in the original comic, I can imagine that there might be some of the taste of Gnosticism coming across. Back then I was trying to express my ideas regarding anarchy. Although I considered anarchy to have a spiritual element as well. I considered it to have a great deal of romanticism in it. And I was interested in occult and Gnostic ideas and there was the 'VI VERI VENIVERSUM VIVUS VICI', the motto from *Faust*, 'through the power of truth, while living, I have conquered the universe.' Yes, it was full of 'V's so it fitted in very nicely, but I liked the sentiments as well. And, yeah, there is a mystical quality to V every bit as much as there is a political one. Because I really do see anarchy as a viable form of political romanticism. I don't see what the hell is wrong with romanticism. It works. And it instils life with something that makes it worth living. It instils it with a spirit. It makes you feel that the world of ideas and spirit is a real and immediate one. So, yeah, in any sort of tract on anarchy, I really did feel impelled to put in a few Gnostic or mystical ideas as well. I mean, the transfiguring or transforming experience that Evey goes through is probably a kind of a brutal form of Gnosticism. A kind of experiencing first hand and knowing it to the depths of your being.

APS: The other was *Marvelman*. I must have been about 17 or 18 when I first discovered it in *Warrior*, and I was reading a lot of Gurdjieff and Ouspensky, and it really hammered home to me the idea of being asleep and waking up, as *Marvelman*'s entire past history was an illusion, a programmed dream that had been set up by Gargunza, and that seems very Gnostic

AM: Well, thank you. I don't know if there was much conscious Gnosticism there. Although, I think that probably I was trying to think of a way in which I didn't have to say, 'And all those illogical *Marvelman* stories from the 1950s didn't happen.' I didn't want to say that because I felt that would have been cheating. So I wanted to come up with a way to explain them. Yes, they did happen, but only in some kind of virtual simulation. I suppose that that idea, well, it wasn't new to me and I had already been reading the work of Philip K Dick, at that point, and so possibly the idea that Marvleman, they've all been kept in a laboratory somewhere, and they all have these sort of adventures in a kind of simulation. That was possibly an idea that I'd had because I was very influenced by Dick. So that was Philip K Dick's Gnosticism, it was probably a kind of second-hand Gnosticism, via Dick, if it was there at all. I did enjoy that series. I've been dealing recently, at second hand, with Mick Anglo, who's still alive and who was always the owner of *Marvelman* apparently. We were lied to. And I'm doing everything that I can, because Mick's very old and he's looking after his very ill wife, and we're trying to help him get

some money for the work he did on *Marvelman*. But there's such a lot of sharks and scumbags circling around the character.

APS: It's an amazingly complicated story isn't it

AM: The thing is, if I hadn't done *Marvelman*, nobody would have been interested in the character because he was a fairly lame knockoff of Captain Marvel, but Mick created him with incredible energy and deserves the credit for it, but there's a lot of people who once they've sniffed that there's a few dollars around have tried to attach themselves to the property, which is why I distanced myself from it and gave all the rights to Neil Gaiman, because I was starting to feel even at that point that it was a poisoned chalice, as much as I enjoyed working upon it, there was something not quite right somewhere.

APS: And is Neil Gaiman supporting Mick Anglo's claim?

AM: As far as I know, yes, the last I heard, me and Neil are both squarely with Mick Anglo, and all of the sharks are trying to claim their share. It's gone to court in Britain, and then in the US, and, I don't know, there are all sorts of exceptions. I've said that I'll write an introduction to a new edition.

APS: And then it'll be published by Marvel who are the ones who vetoed it in the first place.

AM: So we shall see. It's been a trail of tears and I suspect that it isn't over yet. If that answers all your questions, Andrew. It's been a great interview and I look forward to seeing the piece when you've got it done.

APS: Thanks for your time.

AM: My pleasure. You take care of yourself and have a pleasant evening.

William Blake, Laocoön.

Alan Moore

Angel Passage V: Heaven

Into eternity out of one stinking moment. Clocks reversing and the smashed bowl mends, wet salmon-gilded cloud sucked streaming back, inhaled by morning. Time is made a place, made London. Moment windows glinting, decade lanes, and that short Hercules forever stamping in its passages. He is not small, but only far away. He strides through bread riot, match-girl strike, and blitz, through joss-stick parks and dead princess's funeral. We can't keep up with him. He barely keeps up with himself. That headlong charge down twelve streets at a time. He slams through low performance tables, school assembly halls, and rustles chip-wrap at the Proms. He almost runs. Along Museum Street in Duchamp stop-motion with too many arms that raise the hat, tap cane, check pocket-watch, like some fantastic engine, some hallucination, like some slumming Hindu god. Whirlwind litter skyjacked carrier bag his breath, aerosol hiss across election hoarding. Racing, pacing, he sees blossom flaming into slain Nigerian boys in trees at Peckham Rye, and God in Union Jack sunglasses and a guardsman's coat comes barrelling down Carnaby, and peering through a Broad Street window terrifies the child. He's all of him, at once. He barges from the manicurist in South Moulton Street with round the corner handle frowning. Hendrix bucket-splashing vandal sound like paint across the tidy precinct. Boots delighted through the silver scratch card drifts, grabs windfall figs up from his blind guest grave at Bunhill. And from Lambeth out by Waterloo his trains like Behemoth, complaining in the dark. Where by the tracks he's writ great flaming names in spray, the giants of London's quarters now, sees Blad and pest and mane, and there in nude pink letters NoLove, weary Afric titan of the self, and on the high cloud buttered yellow by the moon he'll paint them, soapstone calf and bicep, a cyanic tincture in their modelling, their wide mad eyes stunned by the sun, by love, by tragedy, by everything. And higher still, blown tumbling through the searchlight pillars of a siren night, he sees hot Satan chains of electricity dragged in the lanes below and plunges down into the fireball knot of Soho. He pushes, rude and spluttering, through Les Miserables queues at Leicester Square, and waiting in her bonnet on the ghost of Green Street's corner, takes Kate by the arm, and they duck whispering down confetti alleys. Rent boy cherubs in the tangerine peel and the bubble wrap up Queen Anne's Court. He walks on with his wife, both made from sparks. It's not enough to study or revere him, only be him, kicking down the Greek Street night. And from the frot spots and the lesbo shows, the gleeful orgies of his margins spill into the road. Wet torso clay, lips, limbs and skin, in glistening miles grind yellow in the sodium lights. And smiling, he and Catherine hurry on, order cold mutton in Trattoria's, offer bouncers out, orange and turquoise sparklers in their fists, run up and down the moving stairs of Tottenham Court. Big Issue sailboat-folded for a crown, he's young again and she, and garden-bare they dance the swerving cabs down Oxford Street. He swings her by the waist and everywhere about them flutter cell phones, trilling. The lysergic smear of Russell Square, Huxley and Ginsberg call out to them, giggling and stumbling from the park. Beneath the museum portico he kisses her, and from its vaults reel festivals, parades. Pharaohs and Indian idols with a foam of Soma on their tusks, and alligators crawled up from the Thames, a heavy cancer crust of sapphires creaking on their hides, all teeming in the drunk sloped labyrinth. Time never happened. Past revised unendingly is but the fretful play of mind. We are not jailed by continuity. History's prison bursts, its mortar only spit and wish. We caper outside and away. Now from the galleries and print shops are his fiends and marvels joined with the procession. He and Kate climb naked up astride

Nebuchadnezzar's back and ride him, thumbnails sparking through the torchlight. Here the real and unreal of the ages step together and embrace this place behind the verse, below the colour seeping from the squirrel hair, where wed the flesh and mind, the hand and eye, amongst the antic marriage guests. And in the rice and streamers and the copulation is his vision now descended to him as the woman in his soul who is Jerusalem, the bride, who is the shining city lowering from the firmament. For this is Golgonooza, sand-grained township of eternity, where now comes pleasure sweet Islamic angels as a gem flood pour, comes smiling houris in a streaming radiance, a comet wind. Light fluttering like pages, sound like oil, the ratio transcended in each tree. About him in his nude simplicity, a way to smouldering white, the spectre boil. He rails, divine in tongue but laborious speech, a gentleness more loud than cannon's boom and drafts creation from a tiny room. The universal there in his unique. Hands stained with Paradise or Milton's Fall. He will not let the shock of being fade, but pummelled by the star stands weeping made a boy before the marvel of it all.

> Godiva sky and her atomic blush,
> the trailing peacock hem stained white with flare
> reflects in puddle mud, while everywhere,
> tattooed in heathen gold, the children rush.

And all the wheeling cosmos comes to this, its orbits to an evening's walk pared down. Vast swirls made stains on Catherine's dressing gown and suns careening in the fond, brief kiss. His thumbprint's heat in every just fist curled, in hand on pen, or sharing the last crust. On lovers arse, or tumbling jails to dust, his rages, lusts and fears those of the world. He is our human compass, jumps, limbs splayed to all points, up from the common ground. In fireball dawn, mad glare, torrential sound, is William Blake, amazed and unafraid.

Jim West

Did Moses Really Talk to God?

Did Moses really talk to God? This may seem like a stupid question. But in ancient times this issue was a major subject of controversy among early Christians. This historic controversy is documented extensively in the writings of the Catholic Fathers. And anyone who has studied these writings knows that the New Testament writings were subject to the widest possible interpretations in terms of theology. *Different people read the Gospels and Paul and walked away believing in different gods.* The result was that early Christianity was a deeply divided movement comprised of clamoring theological schools. It is indeed quite fascinating and strange that so many Christians could read these writings and walk away with radically diverse impressions of what these writings said about God. Some readers believed that the Gospels and Paul referred to the Creator God Jehovah as the supreme Being; and others, i.e. the Gnostics, came away equally convinced that a new God was revealed in the same writings. How could something like this happen? Don't the writings of the Apostles make clear who the true God is? Were the Gnostics simply idiots who made spectacular theological errors? Or is there a real theological pattern in these writings that allowed for such radical interpretations?

All history buffs know of course that the Catholic Church ended up victorious in its rivalry against the Gnostics. And whether or not one agrees with the Church's doctrine, one must admit that the Church had a way of making its doctrines stick whether you agreed with it or not. At one time in history it was literally a capital crime not to be a Catholic. This kind of judicial arrangement lasted for over a thousand years and has left a deep impression on the psyche of Western Christians. To this day the theology of 'orthodox' Christianity remains engrained in the culture and thought of most Christians. But whether or not the New Testament writings actually support this theology remains as an unresolved issue.

Today traditional 'orthodox' Christianity has long lost its police-state power. The offices of the Inquisition have been closed… And scholars of all stripes are free to admit that the biblical texts and theology often raise more questions than provide answers. What these writings really tell us, historically, is that the early Christian movement was theologically divided almost from the beginning. Almost from the very beginning Christians did not agree, for example, on whether Moses received the Law from God. Again, traditional ' orthodox' Christianity, going back to the Catholic Fathers, has preached this dogma that Moses spoke to the Most High God, and received the Law there from… but do the earliest ' Apostolic' texts confirm consistently that this is what Jesus taught?

Our first clue showing the nature of this problem is from the Gospel According to John. The following passage is meant to portray the reaction of the Pharisees to the teaching of Jesus:

> We know that God spake unto Moses: as for this fellow, we know not from whence he is. (Jn. 9:29)

The Pharisees understood Jesus to mean that Moses was not in contact with the supreme Being. There are other passages in John which support this interpretation. For example, in John

17:25 Jesus says: ' O righteous Father, the world has not known you.' (Jn. 17:25, cf. Isaiah 64:4)

And also from Jesus in John 6:46, ' Not that any man has seen the Father, save he who is from God.' (Jn. 6:46, cf. 6:45, Isaiah 54:13, 6:1ff.)

And also the words of John the Baptist in John 1:17-18, ' For the law was given by Moses, but grace and truth came by Jesus Christ. No man has seen God at any time.'

And also the words of John the Apostle, in 1 John 4:12, 'No man has seen God at any time. If we love one another, God dwells in us, and his love is perfected in us.'

The passages above reflect a pattern in Jesus' teaching which involves the revelation of some other God aside from the God revealed through Moses. Here again is an example from the Gospel of Matthew where Jesus proclaims to the Jews: 'No man knoweth the Son but the Father; neither knoweth any man the Father save the Son, and he to whomsoever the Son will reveal him.' (Mt. 11:27)

According to these words Moses knew neither the Son nor the Father.

And again from the Gospel of Luke: 'But love your enemies…and your reward shall be great, and ye shall be children of the Highest: for he is kind unto the unthankful and the evil.' (Lk. 6:35)

For the discerning reader there is no doubt that the passages above represent some other theological consensus quite contrary to the consensus mandated by Christian 'orthodox' tradition. Now certainly there are passages in the New Testament Gospels that do reflect the 'orthodox' consensus (e.g. Mt. 15:4, Lk. 4:8). I will not deny this. But the relevant question is why do the four Gospels lack a consistent theology? The passages above cannot be reconciled with any traditional, linear theology which attempts to trace the revelation of God back to Moses.

Just for the sake of reference let us look at some key passages from the books of Moses on which the 'orthodox' theology is based. Deuteronomy 34:10 provides an excellent example: 'And there arose not a prophet since in Israel like unto Moses, whom YHWH knew face to face.'

And also Deuteronomy 5:2-4, 'The Lord our God made a covenant with us in Horeb. The Lord made not this covenant with out Fathers, but with us, even us, who are all of us here alive this day. The Lord (YHWH) talked with you face to face in the mount out of the midst of the fire…'

And then there is Exodus 20:22, 'And YHWH said unto Moses, Thus you shall say unto the children of Israel, 'Ye have seen that I have talked with you from heaven…''

Can these passages cited above, from the Old and New Testaments, be reconciled? Any reasonable person would have to admit that the answer is *No*. The reality is that there was some segment of the earliest Christians who believed that Jesus disclosed the existence of some other God. This sublime theme, and its implications, are most obvious in the passage in Luke 6:35b, where we are informed that the 'Highest' God is '*kind unto the unthankful and the evil*.' These words can in no way be reconciled with the judicial standard as reported in the Law of Moses. In the Law we learn that the Lord is a 'jealous' God who will severely punish transgressions: '*For you shall fear the Lord your God and serve him…lest the anger of the Lord your God be kindled against you, and destroy ye from off the face of the earth*' (Dt. 6:13, 15). And Numbers 14 provides a record of how the Lord punished the Israelites for their murmurings and ingratitude. Again, this cannot be reconciled with the words in Luke 6:35. The overall implication of this passage in Luke is that the judicial standard of the Law of Moses is not connected with the true God. And the statement is more than likely the reflection of a criticism of the Old Testament and its brutality and violence. Hence Jesus commanded his followers to '*love their enemies*' whereas the God of Moses commanded his followers to '*show no mercy*' (Dt. 7:2; cf. 2:34, 3:6, 23:1-3).

If Moses was not talking to God, then who was he talking to? Believe it or not, the New Testament writings provide an answer here too—if you can set aside all of the orthodox propaganda which has for so long led readers to overlook the obvious.

In Galatians 3:19 St. Paul informs his readers that the Law was '*ordained by angels*' (in Greek: *diatageis di' aggelon*). In the same text Paul warned his readers that no one should believe any other gospel aside from the Gospel of Liberty preached by Paul (cf. 2 Cor. 3:17). Hence Paul warned his readers: '*But though we, or an angel (aggelos) from heaven, preach any other gospel than that which we have preached unto you, let him be accursed (anathema)*' (Gal. 1:8). Orthodox leaders have used Paul's rhetoric here as a sanction to enforce their own theological

mandates, and to condemn anyone who held different views. But in reality Paul's caustic language was directed against Jewish Christian adversaries who were condemning him, and who insisted that all non-Jewish converts must obey the Law of Moses. This is what Paul's 'anathema' was directed against. In this context Paul insisted instead that the Law was ordained by angels; and he issued the following warning to any Christians who followed the teaching of the Jewish faction: '*You have become strangers to Christ. Whosoever of you are justified by the Law, ye are fallen from grace*' (Gal. 5:4).

Paul's main point in this letter was to persuade his readers that God could not be known or served through the Law: '*When ye knew not God ye did service to those which by nature are no gods. But now, after ye have known God, or rather are known by God, why turn you again to the inferior elements, whereunto you desire again to be in bondage? Ye observe days and months and times and years*' (Gal. 4:8-10). In these words Paul reveals his opinion that the Mosaic tradition is just another form of the worship of the celestial bodies, which the pagans called 'gods' and the Jews called 'angels.' Paul here denies that the Law of Moses is connected with God.

The fact that Paul rejected the God of Mosaic tradition is clearly implied in these words from 1 Corinthians 10:18-19, '*Behold Israel after the flesh: are not they which eat of the sacrifices partakers of the alter? What say I then? That the idol is anything, or that which is offered in sacrifice to idols is anything?*'

Let he who has eyes, read and understand…

My point in all this is that Paul, in his letters, preserves an element of that obscure teaching that is attributed to Jesus as quoted above. Jesus's God is not the God of the Law: Paul tells us that the 'Law' was 'ordained by angels.' Hence, Jesus reveals the true God, whereas Moses spoke on behalf of certain angels.

So where did Paul learn this doctrine? Paul tells his readers that he learned it from the risen Christ alone, and not from any 'flesh and blood' man (Gal. 1:11-16). Paul may be telling the truth; although I suspect that his real goal in saying this was to set some distance between himself and the Jewish Apostles at Jerusalem, i.e. Peter, John, James, et al. (Gal. 2:1-11). Otherwise there is evidence that there were other members of the early Christian movement *before Paul* who also taught the same doctrine, and were probably the source of Paul's ideas. I refer in this case to St. Stephen in the book of Acts, who was an outstanding member of the Hellenist wing of the early Church at Jerusalem. Stephen taught a doctrine remarkably similar to the doctrine taught later by Paul. According to Acts Paul's first contact with Stephen was on the day of the latter's execution; which was carried out by the Jewish Council on a charge of blasphemy (Acts 6:11, 7:53-8:1). Paul (or 'Saul') later converted to Christianity and taught a similar doctrine.

Before I get ino the charges against Stephen, and the nature of his doctrine, I want to establish some parameters regarding the book of Acts. In general I do not believe that this book is a trustworthy account of the early Church. This account represents an idealized picture of the early Church which was put together with the aim of portraying Paul and the Jewish Apostles (Peter, et al.) as unified, and that Paul submitted to the '12.' Paul's letters of course indicate the opposite on all counts; but we can't get into that here. I do believe that there is a general pattern of truth in Acts, and there are some elements of an authentic tradition preserved. I believe that the account of Stephen is an example, and is based on something that really happened. This account also shows an early unorthodox theology that was embraced by the Hellenist wing of the early church, which included Stephen, Philip, Nicolas and Simon Magus, and, inevitably, Paul.

Of note is that the latter four names all have some legacy in Gnostic tradition. My immediate aim is to show that the Stephen account in Acts may show an historic precedent for the emergence of Gnostic theology and its origins in earliest Christian circles.

Acts 6:11 tells us that Stephen was accused of speaking 'blasphemous words against Moses and against God' on account of his preaching in local Hellenist-Jewish synagogue (6:9). Stephen is brought to trial accordingly before the Jewish religious council. Before the council Stephen is portrayed as giving a lengthy speech which describes the history of the biblical patriarchs. This speech is probably in some part a production of the writer. Yet there are certain elements here which are not consistent with the overall theology of Acts. The speech starts out as conventional in nature; but then, all of a sudden, 'Stephen' says that 'Moses' receive the Law, viz., the 'living oracles', from an 'angel' on Mt. Sinai (Acts 7:37-39; 7:53). Stephen also denies that God commanded King Solomon to build the Temple: 'But Solomon built him a House. Howbeit the Most High dwelleth not in temples made with hands' (7:47-48). The Old Testament tells us much to the contrary that 'God' did command that Solomon build the Temple; and that King David was barred from this task because of the violence of his reign (2 Samuel 7:12-14, 1 Kings 5:3-5, 1 Chron. 28:3). Thus Stephen's version of history and theology, as reported in Acts, does not coincide with the Old Testament. This deviation appears once again at the end of Stephen's speech, where he declares that the forefathers 'received the law by the disposition of angels' (*diatagas aggelon*) and 'have not kept it' (Acts 7:53). It is following these very words that the Jewish authorities were 'furious and gnashed at him with their teeth' (verse 54). Stephen was dragged out and stoned while 'Saul' watched.

I can't help but wonder if this account of Stephen is based on an eye-witness report of his trial. There are numerous details in this speech that would have gotten Stephen thrown out of the Nicene Council, or burned at the stake by the Inquisition. Why would the orthodox leaning author/editor of Acts simply make all this up? Perhaps the reason is that this account is based on an authentic written report which in turn may be the earliest authentic account to survive from the earliest Christians—and which records events that occurred *before Paul's conversion*. This early record shows a profile of an early Greek-speaking Jewish-Christian who denied the traditional biblical theology of Judaism at certain key points. Stephen denied that Moses spoke to God on Mt. Sinai, and said instead that the Law was ordered by angels, using the same basic words as used by Paul later in Gal. 3:19 (Paul: *diatageis di' aggelon*; Stephen: *diatagas aggelon*). Stephen also denied that God ordered the Temple at Jerusalem. Stephen's theology resembles later Gnostic theology, which also denied that the supreme Being had any direct role in the Old Testament. And certainly there are historic links between Stephen's fellow Hellenists and the later Gnostic movement. The Catholic Fathers accused both Simon Magus and Nicolas of being inventors of heresies. A Gnostic 'gospel' is named after Philip. And the Gnostics were known to lay claim to Paul as one of their own. All of these men were members of the Hellenist wing of the original church at Jerusalem.

I should also point out here that there is a subtle distinction in Acts between the 'Hebrew' and 'Hellenist' Christians (all being Jews). This division is indicated in Acts 6 where we learn that there is a conflict between the *Hebrews* and *Hellenists* over the feeding of the widows (6:1). The friction surely ran deeper than that; but it is the purpose of our writer to smooth these conflicts over. Yet the Acts account inevitably reports that the great persecution, caused by Stephen's blasphemy, did not include the Jewish Apostles, and that they remained in Jerusalem unmolested (8:1). The reality behind this is that the Jewish Church (the Hebrews) was not the target of this persecution. Only the Hellenists

were targeted. And nowhere in Acts is Peter or any of the Apostles accused of the offenses that Stephen was. Peter and the Apostles were accused of preaching 'Jesus' as Messiah, which was a political offense (e.g. Acts 5:26-42). Paul is portrayed in Acts as persecuting all Christians, and that all Christians feared him even after his conversion (8:3, 9:26). But Paul himself reports that none of the Jewish Christians recognized him when he went to Jerusalem (Gal. 1:22; 2:1-10). Paul's account and the Acts account cannot be reconciled. These subtle points indicate that the Hellenist Church was the source of the 'heretical' theology that appeared with Stephen, Paul, Simon and Nicolas. Again, all of these men have some place in Gnostic tradition; and their doctrine agrees with the Gnostics in that Moses does not represent the supreme Being. Hence *Moses did not talk to God*.

This theme regarding Moses also resonates with certain statements attributed to Jesus in the Gospels as I have shown above. There are other New Testament sources which reflect this doctrine. Hebrews 2:2f. says that the Law of Moses is the '*word spoken by angels*' whereas salvation was first spoken of by the Lord, with 'God' bearing witness with 'signs and wonders.' And in Colossians 2:13-18 the Law of Moses is equated with the '*worshipping of angels*' (verse 18). This is all part of an obscure circle of theological ideas which has only been fully realized in the historic Gnostic movement; whereas orthodox Christianity has clung to its own Hellenistic version of a Jewish theology. The New Testament Gospels and the Letters of Paul in fact preserve the elements of both theologies. (Orthodox tampering is surely the cause of this.)

Now of course there is one important question which can be raised against my arguments: If Paul and Stephen truly rejected the notion that Moses spoke to God, then why do these men still teach that God appeared to Abraham, which is a lesson taught by Moses?

This question leads to the consideration of some very important issues—especially in regard to Paul. It is true that Paul taught that God appeared to Abraham. But it is also important to note that there are significant differences between Paul's account of Abraham and that attributed to Moses in Genesis 17. In the latter we are told that 'God' gave the rite of circumcision to Moses as a 'sign of the Covenant' (Gen. 17:10-11). Paul, on the other hand, denies that God gave the rite of circumcision to Abraham, and says instead that Abraham was justified by his faith (Gal. 3:6-9). But this is not what Genesis 17 says. The latter states that Abraham and all his descendants must be circumcised if they want to be heirs to the Covenant: 'And the uncircumcised man child whose flesh of his foreskin is not circumcised, that soul shall be cut off from his people; he hath broken my covenant' (Gen. 17:14). Paul argues the opposite and says that Abraham and his children were justified by faith alone (Gal. 3:6-9, 18). Again, Genesis 17 states that God gave 'circumcision' to Abraham, and his descendants, as a sign of his faith: whereas Paul says that Abraham was 'justified' by his faith, and no circumcision was required of him or his children. Paul assigns circumcision to the Law of Moses, and not to the covenant, or 'promise', made to Abraham.

In the example above it is obvious that Paul has made an argument which has no basis in scripture, and actually opposes the scriptural account. The implication here is that Paul did not accept the books of Moses as an authoritative account of history and theology. Paul's ideas are based on some other *counter-tradition*. Another example is where Paul wrote that the Law was *ordained by angels*: but again, this is not what the books of Moses say. Paul's doctrine originates from some other tradition and system of theology. It is not Bible based as we know it.

We may certainly understand Paul to mean that Moses misrepresented Abraham's doctrine and theology, and that Paul is correcting this on the basis of some other tradition. Of note is that in 2 Corinthians 3:12-4:4 Paul bluntly accuses Moses of blinding the minds of the Israelites. Moses is said to have worn a veil in order to conceal the 'fading glory' of the Lawgiver; whereas the true glory and the true salvation are revealed in the open face of Jesus Christ…

In the case of Stephen there is a notable contradiction on the issue of Abraham and circumcision. In contrast with Paul 'Stephen' affirms that God gave the rite of circumcision to Abraham (Acts 7:8). But it is highly probable that this part of the speech was constructed by the author of Acts: whereas the later unorthodox elements of the speech were based on real sources—and are supported by the later writings of Paul. I believe it is highly probable that Paul's writings provide the most reliable and complete representation of Stephen's doctrine; whereas Acts preserves only part of it.

All of the evidence I have shown above; from the Gospels, Stephen and Paul, show that there was some other theological tradition that existed among the earliest Christians. Not all of them placed priority on the Mosaic tradition, and the notion that God spoke to Moses *face to face*.

Luke Valentine

How Many Worlds Do We Exist in Simultaneously?

The Owl in the Daylight and the Life of Philip K. Dick

INT.—LIVING ROOM—1974. The silhouette of Philip K. Dick completely in shadow dominates the screen. He appears to be passionately listening to the scherzo from the second movement of Beethoven's ninth symphony. Quick cuts of his dissheveled southern California living room and writing desk in disarray, home to both a SF pulp writer and crash pad of numerous others, vacant now save for the crushed cigarette and empty glass detritus of their most recent romp. The doorbell rings. LIGHT falls on his figure and face. He is writhing in pain. The bell rings again and startles him. CUT to INT.—LIVING ROOM DOOR—CLOSED. The bell rings once more, and Dick's hand opens the door revealing the figure of a young woman in silhouette, light pouring from behind her. As the doo opens FOCUS on the woman. She is young and dark haired and is making a drug store delivery.

DELIVERY WOMAN: Mr. Dick? You called about the pain?

DICK (looking into the woman's eyes, then perplexedly on her gold necklace, an Icthyus dangling from it catching the light): What is that necklace you're wearing?

DELIVERY WOMAN: It's called an Icthyus. It's a symbol from ancient Rome. The early Christians used it to recognize one another.

Dick continues to gaze at the Icthyus as a bright pink light emanates from it coloring everything. Dick squints finally closing his eyes. FADE TO BLACK.

The nature of identity is one of the great themes of postmodern writing. Philip K.

Dick's writing has been reconsidered of late as belonging to a more literary genre than the pop SF cult pulps he was thought to have cranked out during his lifetime. A prestigious Library of America edition of four Dick novels was published in the spring of 2007 and a second edition is scheduled for release on July 31. His reviews are far more glowing now than they ever were in his lifetime. But critics unfamiliar with Dick's transformative mystical experiences and religious works, such as his *Tractates Cryptica Scriptura* and two million word *Exegesis*, often miss the point.

Dick's quest for identity is far more than clever artistic trickery begging for deconstruction. It belongs to a realm that transcends time and space, and though Dick found himself working with one of the great themes of his or any other day, pulling from his writer's toolbox point-of-view and perspectival techniques of the postmodern period, he was coming from and going to other directions entirely. His inspiration was more than literary. His was divine.

Today, Dick is most widely known as the original writer of the stories behind the films *Blade Runner*, *Total Recall*, *Minority Report*, *A Scanner Darkly*, and the recent *Next*. Inventive and prolific, he left us with the beginning of an unfinished novel he called *The Owl in Daylight*.

The Owl in Daylight is also part of the story of a Philip K. Dick film biography set for release in 2009. Toni Grisoni whose credits include *Fear and Loathing in Las Vegas* is writing the screenplay for Electric Shepherd, the creative production arm of the Philip K. Dick Estate. Paul Giamotti (nominated for an academy award for best supporting actor in *Cinderella Man*) will portray the revered author and mystic.

Grisoni is interweaving Dick's life and his mystical experiences with Dick's plot for *The Owl in Daylight*, Giamotti told MTV Movie News, 'The idea is to take one of his last stories and put him as a character in the story. A lot of his stories were about reality getting bent around, so we're trying to do that.'

Dick began writing science fiction short stories in 1951 for the many pulp SF magazines such as *If*, *Galaxy*, and *Amazing Stories* popular at the time. His ambitions though included mainstream realist novels. 'I knew all kinds of people who were doing literary-type novels,' he is quoted in his chronology appended to the Library of America edition of four of his novels. 'They all encouraged me to write, but there was no encouragement to sell anything. But I wanted to sell, and I also wanted to do science fiction. My ultimate dream was to be able to do both literary stuff and science fiction.' He concentrated on science fiction for a few years, then turned his hand to realist novels. Few of his realist works were published. Though they were largely unnoticed, he applied the skills he honed writing them to science fiction, publishing in 1958 his first U.S. hardcover, *Time Out of Joint*. *Time Out of Joint* billed itself not as science fiction, but as 'a novel of menace'.

In 1961, after discovering the *I Ching*, Dick began writing *The Man in the High Castle*, an alternate reality tale, published as a 'thriller'. He used the *I Ching* to help plot it out. 'I thought I had bridged the gap between the experimental mainstream novel and science fiction,' he said. The next year his agency returned fully ten realist manuscripts it considered unsaleable. Then in September, *The Man in the High Castle* won the most prestigious prize in scifidom, the Hugo Award. His reputation and income from his writing derived mainly from his short stories in the pulps, and with the Hugo, he was forever stereotyped as a writer of science fiction in the minds of the publishing world.

EXT. - FIRST CENTURY ROME - A CROWDED ROMAN MARKETPLACE - DAY. Philip K. Dick, attired as a poor Roman artisan, is frantically running from a pair of Roman soldiers. They almost apprehend him, but he pushes over a basket of fish and gets away. The Roman soldiers slip on the fish, and one of them falls in the street. He runs down an alley to a doorway and knocks weakly at the door as he slouches on it. He puts his hand to his side and sees that he is bleeding. He looks up and sees the Roman soldiers searching the street outside the alley. He knocks again, louder. A shadowy figure opens the door and pulls him in as the camera pans up to an Icythus symbol carved in stone above the door.

What did Dick see in the pink beam of light that radiated from the Icythus dangling from the delivery woman's necklace? Much more than his perception of having been a persecuted Christian two thousand years before. Throughout the remainder of his life, he would work almost daily on his *Exegesis* in which he explored that and similiar experiences after the bell rang in 1974. For the rest of his life, even during those rare periods when he wasn't composing fiction on his white Olympic typewriter using only his two blazingly fast index fingers, Dick undertook, in the *Exegesis* to understand mentally and spiritually the pink beam and following visions of February and March 1974. Referring to his visionary insights as '2-3-74', he came to realize that he could never fully comprehend the profoundly paradoxical and multiple meanings revealed to him. But before he died, he left the world with ten thousand pages of rough draft, some typewritten, some handwritten, in the *Exegesis*.

Unless one reads Dick's constant reiterations and musings of meaning, much of the *Exegesis* seems self-assured. ''Salvation' through gnosis— more properly amamnesis (the loss of amnesia)— although it has individual significance for each of us—a quantum leap in perception, identity, cognition, understanding, world—and self-experience, including immortality—it has greater and further importance for the system as a whole, inasmuch as these memories are data needed by it and valuable to it, to its overall functioning.' The world that is taken to be real, read by the senses and written by the mind is 'a cardboard, a fake.' Gnosis is in recognizing the false, ignoring the illusions, and above all, seeing/remembering the system of divinity that connects us all.

Even his fans were sometimes dumbfounded by some of Dick's statements on the subject of his own not always in the present identity. In France in 1977, delivering the keynote address at an SF convention called 'If You Find This World Bad, You Should See Some of the Others', Dick said that two of his novels, *The Man in the High Castle* and the critically well received *Flow My Tears, the Policeman Said* were based on his jagged memories of a slave state world. Stunned, the audience left the auditorium with eyes like saucers and mouths agape.

'Reality, to me, is not so much something that you perceive, but something you make,' he said in 'The Android and the Human'. The truth behind reality is 'what you do with the bits and pieces of meaningless, puzzling, disappointing, even cruel and crushing fragments all around us that seem to be pieces left over, discarded, from another world entirely that did, maybe, make sense.'

Another, far more concise, theophilosophical work is appended to *VALIS*, a SF novel in which he fictionalizes 2-3-74 (fictionalization in Dick's case usually being more like bringing the reality of his life into a blurry focus). There Dick summarized his *Exegesis* in *Tractates Cryptica Scriptura*. Reality is an illusion, a prison in which we are trapped. Not a prison of our own making, but one from which, to break free, we must awaken to our true natures.

FLASH FORWARD TO 1982. 'Its a folk expression from the South—an owl being blind in the daylight,' Dick said in an interview with Gwen Lee, one of the last interviews of his life. It simply means a person whose judgement is clouded over. The book is about the inability to understand. I can't even put it into words.'

Inspired while listening to soul lifting strains of Beethoven, Dick conceived for *The Owl in Daylight* a world of humanoids in the far reaches of space with no ability to hear or detect sound and whose only sensory information about the universe comes from their hyperdeveloped sense of sight. They can see how things appear in most all of the light spectrum—x-rays and gamma rays, for example—unlike terrestial humans who can only see a tiny sliver of the light spectrum with the eye. Having no auditory capacity, the insightful but mute aliens communicate through colour frequencies rather than sound frequencies such as those generated by our vocal chords.

Dick's interview with Lee is transcribed in *What If Our World Is Their Heaven?: The Last Conversations of Philip K. Dick* published by OverLook Press and co-authored by Doris Sauter. Lee was a close friend of Doris's, Dick's neighbor and long-time friend, as well as with Dick's then fifteen year old daughter, Isa. Lee was an aspiring journalist and writer. She recorded a series of interviews with Dick, the last of which was held just two weeks before the stroke that ended Dick's life in 1982—only four months before the release of *Blade Runner*, the first film based on a Dick story, to put it in perspective. Among Lee's interview notes is an outline in miniature of the whole story of *The Owl in Daylight* along with Dick's development of the story.

'It would begin on another star system on a planet with a civilization quite different from ours—a civilization where there's no atmosphere such as we have and as a result, speech is never developed; they're mute and deaf. And because of the failure to utilize sound, they have no art predicated on sound.'

Their inability to know sound, however, makes the effects of sound seem mystical and awe inspiring to them. 'And what I want to do is, you know,' Dick explained, 'the way we have in our world mystical visions of heaven, like at the end of Dante's Divine Comedy, and these visions are generally that heaven is light—the concept of light is almost always associated with the next world to us.' Despite their hyperfamiliarity with all things revealed by any natural light, or maybe because of it, their glances (so to speak) of the mystery of sound in the universe fascinate them to the point of reverence. 'Their normal world would be the way we envision the next world to be,' said Dick.

Some of the deaf humanoids have visions of Earth and our experience with sound. A few of them travel to Earth from their far off world. The occular aliens waylay a successful B movie music composer, one Ed Firmley, and implant a biochip in his head through which they plan to broadcast Ed Firmley's flourishing experiences of sound back to the home planet. Dick continues in his interview with Lee extensively on *Owl*. But the novel was never finished, and the story was never told.

Until now. Not as a novel, but as a screenplay. And not as Dick's last story. At least not as such. Grisoni is bending the story of Dick's life around the character of Ed Firmley, if Giamotti's statement about 'bending reality' is any clue. Readers of *VALIS* remember some point-of-view shape shifting between the main character, Horselover Fat, and the actual writer, Philip K. Dick. Philip K. Dick the writer bent himself around Horselover Fat the narrator in *VALIS*, not by a shift in narrational points of view, but by the real Philip K. Dick finding himself in the fictional body of his character Horselover Fat, narrating in the character's stead. The artistic effect of this technique is that of reality entering a world that doesn't really exist.

Narrating as Dick-as-Horselover Fat in *VALIS*, Dick wrote, 'If it wasn't for Horselover Fat and his encounter with God or Zebra or the Logos, and this other person living in Fat's head but in another century and place, I would dismiss my dreams as nothing...Dreams of another life? But where?..Are we all like Horselover Fat, but don't know it? How many worlds do we exist in simultaneously?' Dick deftly blends the unreal fictional world with the world of reality until the fictional world becomes more real and the real world of Philip K. Dick and ourselves less so.

Electric Shepherd is owned by the Philip K. Dick Estate, which is to say by his children. In addition to Isa, there is Laura (Dick) Leslie and Dick's son, Chris. After Dick's death, Isa and Lee Gwen remained friends and Lee became closer with the younger Laura as well. The production company was set up by the Dick children in 2005 after their disappointment with the films *Screamers* and *Paycheck* based on Dick stories so that the daughters could take 'a stronger hand in future projects' according to a September story in the LA Times. In October, Electric Shepherd announced that they had negotiated with The Halcyon Company, a start-up production company, to allow them to have the first crack at any PKD related Electric Shepherd project.

'Our Father's library and legacy are deeply important to us and we will strive to bring the highest level of integrity to each project we produce,' said Isa and Laura in a press release announcing the arrangement.

Overlook Press is now disputing Electric Shepherd's rights to *The Owl in Daylight* based on their publication of *What If Our World Is Their Heaven* and to Gwen Lee's notes from her interviews with Dick. Whether OverLook has any claim to movie rights is the sort of question that causes Hollywood producers and their lawyers to generate radioactive Blackberry waves, given that the story was Dick's and Lee was essentially taking notes. Then there's the way Dick wrote. His stories would go through numerous changes in their conception, he never used an outline, and he sometimes grafted entire other stories onto his current project, doing the composing in a non-stop matter of days. In an interview with Gregg Rickmann, Dick says he wanted to use the title for a realist novel. Based on her conversations with Dick, Lee concludes that he liked the title and the Faustian theme he wanted to use for it, and by the time of her interview that he had decided to write it as science fiction. Lee's is one of the few, and certainly the latest, sources of information about the unfinished novel. The dispute is being acted out through the companies and Lee and Sauter and the Dick daughters, have remarkably remained friends, though they do not to talk to each other on the matter directly.

MONTAGE: A series of newspapers swirl, the last remaining static with the Variety headline: 'CHICKS NIX DICKS FLICKS'.

Flicks? Yes there are two of them. As always with anything Philip K. Dick, the story takes yet another bizarre turn. An unrelated project depicting Dick's life premiered in Las Vegas on Friday the thirteenth of June. Released as *Your Name Here*, the film uses the same technique of interposing scenes from Dick's life and his stories. *Your Name Here* stars Bill Pullman (he was the president in *Independence Day*) as a writer based on Philip K. Dick but, to avoid hassles over who owns the rights to Dick's life, not (wink, nudge) based on Philip K. Dick. Directed by Matthew Wilder, the musician, *Your Name Here* is his first directorial attempt. The production goes out of its way to detach itself from any legal reference to Philip K. Dick or *The Owl in Daylight*, though not very far out given the obvious references in *Your Name Here* to Dick. Pullman plays the character with a Dickish beard and the Dick-but-not-Dick character is named Frick—a hybrid of Dick and Frimley.

Taryn Manning co-stars with Pullman as a Victoria Principal based character with whom Dick was, she says to MTV Movie News, obsessed. 'All around his office you see pictures of me. One day, he does a huge line, and the next thing you know he's in the back of a limo, and there I am!' Manning said.

Pullman's character in *Your Name Here* is driven by schizophrenia, speed, and obsession over the actress based on Principal. It is true that Dick's prolificacy was aided for a number of years by prescription amphetamines and to some he exhibited paranoia off the DSM-IV chart. *Your Name Here* highlights the over ballyhooed drug usage aspect of Dick's life. Pullman as Frick seems to have a bottle of Scotch in front of him in most of the released stills.

The Internet Movie Database (IMDb) confirms Manning's version: *Your Name Here* tells the tale of the Sci-fi author William J. Frick during the last few days of his life. Penniless and living in squalor, Bill Frick is on a mission to finish his latest literary masterpiece. His inspiration is the actress Nikki Principal: the object of his obsession. After evading a lengthy visit from an IRS agent, Bill has a sudden stroke and wakes up in a limo with none other than Nikki Principal herself, who informs him that his current literary endeavor is going to change the world. He looks out his window and soon realizes that he has become a God amongst mortals, as murals and statues of him permeate the entire city. The vast majority of people worship him, but some like the nefarious Maurice Kroger want Bill's knowledge and power for their own malicious agenda. Over time Bill realizes that he is now living in a world in which he created, he is living one of his novels.'

In an interview with Wilder by Cal Kemp on Collider.com, Kemp observes that the lead character in *Your Name Here* 'obviously' comes from Philip K. Dick. He then asks Wilder if Wilder is a fan of Dick's. Wilder responds, 'No, I wouldn't say that. This has been a big bone of contention, the Philip K. Dickness of this. This was always intended to be a very fictional movie.'

Both *The Owl in Daylight* and *Your Name Here* are so similiar in premise, studio argumentation over infringement might seem likely. Legally speaking, Dick is dead and no one owns the right to tell his biography. The use of Dick's stories by way of the contrapuntal real life/fictional life technique is another matter. With Dick's life so much a part of his writing, possessing it like a spirit beyond exorcism, it is hard to imagine it being told any other way and still getting it right.

Production of *The Owl in Daylight* now seems to have shifted to legal offices until the copyright issue is resolved. But which of the two films will capture Philip K. Dick? Dick is hard to pin down by anyone, whether moviemaker, literary critic, or avid reader. The lit crits sometimes accuse Dick of a cardinal sin in the fictional world, that of using the forbidden deux ex machina technique in the wormholes of his narrative action. Again, they miss the point. Dick's deux ex machina is a merciless mechanistic universe that eats up and spits out humans back into the worlds in which they find themselves trapped. Rather, the technique he most effectively employed is the mise en abyme, an infinte iteration, as though Dick and his protagonists are mirrors forever reflecting each other, each new iteration contained within itself smaller and smaller until Dick turns to another protagonist and the process repeats ad infinitum.

To Dick, the universe is a machine and there is a god in it—though not the God he matched wits with in the *Exegesis*. He tried mightily to reconcile his own identity with what happened to him in 2-3-74 with the real God in the universal machine. God answered all the permutations of data Dick served up in this game of cosmic I/O and when God crunched Dick's numbers, His answer was always the same.

'I am the doubter and the doubt,' said Dick, and God answered, '...I have equated infinity with me. What, then, is the chance that it is me? You are not the doubter you are doubt itself...You cannot be positive, you will doubt. But what is your guess?'

Dick replied, 'Probably it is you since there is an infinity of infinities forming before me.' And God answered, 'There is the answer, the only one you will ever have.'

DICK: You could be pretending to be God.

GOD: Infinity.

DICK: You could be testing out a logic system in a giant computer and I am...

GOD: Infinity.

DICK: Will it always be an infinity?

GOD: Try further.

DICK: I doubt if you exist.

GOD: Infinity. I will play this game forever.

The reality that Dick tried so hard and through so much pain to understand and explain always eluded him, as it always eludes us. Ultimately Dick despaired that, despite his mighty effort, he was unable to understand, intellectually, his powerful encounters with a true reality. Commenting on his 1976 short story, 'Second Variety', he stated his 'grand theme' as 'Who is human and who

only appears (masquerades) as human?' And though Dick himself may never have understood the mystical reality he experienced, through his very many words, he did explain a transcendent reality to his knowing and careful readers—the real truth of human existence: To be a real human is to be many humans at once, often in surprising and baffling ways, day after day after day.

Everyone connected with the *The Owl in Daylight* may benefit in a year or two. Having more than one movie out on the same subject has happened before, and with *Your Name Here* recently released and *Owl* pushed back, the spectacle of two Dicks played by two different actors in two different movies at the same time has faded. Dick's daughters, through Electric Shepherd in their deal with Halcyon, aim to see their father's work receive worthy screen treatments, and also keep his written word alive in print. Dick's now glowing literary reputation and still growing readership are thanks in large part to their work through Electric Shepherd and the Estate. Gwen Lee and her publisher will at least see increased orders of *What If Our World is Their Heaven?* among Dick's fanatic SF legions and can count on interviews and exposure when *Owl* is released. Doris Sauter is at work on a book about Dick of her own. Among the women, the tone and intent of talks likely weigh heavier than the outcome of financial squabbling among the publishers and production companies when it comes to preserving long-time friendships. Everyone gets something along the glistening tinseled avenues of Hollywood.

Unless, of course, you're Philip K. Dick. One minute, you're sitting at your typewriter listening to Ludwig and banging out a potboiler for which you've already been paid and your agent has already asked you will it work, and the next minute the director yells, 'Sound!' and you're melting in the blinding glare of Kleig lights in makeup and costume and you're a fictional character named Frick or Frimley or Dick or something like that when in reality you're not an actor or a character in a movie or in a book, or even a cult SF writer, for God's sake.

The Second Coming of Freke and Gandy

QUESTIONS AND ANSWERS

***The Gospel of the Second Coming* is described as 'a post-modern Gnostic gospel for the 21st century'. What does that mean?**

FREKE & GANDY: The Gnostics were early Christians who wrote a large number of gospels in which they put their words into Jesus' mouth. It was a common practise in the ancient world to write such works of spiritual fiction. Our new book is a post-modern version of a Gnostic gospel.

Were the Gnostics heretics?

FREKE & GANDY: The Roman Church labelled the Gnostics as heretics and persecuted them out of existence; but with the discovery of a library of Gnostic gospels in Egypt in the last century, we discovered that actually the Gnostics were the original Christians and the Roman Church were the heretics who perverted the true message of Christianity. We have previously written a number of more academic books exploring this idea, which is increasingly been adopted by other open-minded scholars.

On the cover your book is claimed to be 'irreverently serious and profoundly satirical'— can a book be both serious and funny?

FREKE & GANDY: Why not? Life itself is both serious and funny. Our new book is a romp through history, mythology and philosophy, which combines fact and fiction. It aims to be an enjoyable read, but it also makes some very important points about what happened in the past and the nature of the present moment. It draws on the years of research that went into our more academic books, to present a complete revision of our understanding of Christianity in a fun and accessible way.

What's so controversial about the contents of your book?

FREKE & GANDY: Just about everything! We show that the Jesus story found in the New Testament is a myth based on previous Pagan myths of a dying and resurrecting godman; there never was an historical Jesus, because he is the hero of an allegorical fable created by the Gnostics - the whole Jesus story is itself one big parable, which encodes the spiritual teachings that lead to the state of mystical enlightenment, which the original Christians called 'gnosis'.

What is gnosis?

FREKE & GANDY: Gnosis is a state of spiritual awakening in which you realise that in reality all is one. *The Gospel of the Second Coming* is a spiritual fable in which Jesus reveals the secrets of gnosis. And he really does an excellent job. It's mind-blowing stuff!

What made you write a new gospel?

FREKE & GANDY: We felt that a lot of people were getting bored of the old ones. On top of which, the Gnostics taught that the way to show you had understood the gnosis was by writing your own gospel, so we thought we'd have a go. Luckily we managed to talk Jesus into reprising his starring role. That was a bit of an unexpected coup, because we had no idea he was such a big fan of our previous books. Once we'd got Jesus on board we knew we had a potential bestseller on our hands.

What was it like working with Jesus?

FREKE & GANDY: He wasn't nearly as stuffy as we'd expected. We had to put up with the occasional tantrum, but you accept that from the really big stars. He's under a lot of pressure. He obviously struggles with being the son of such a famous father. Plus the fan mail is overwhelming and the requests to do charity benefits never stop. Not that he actually reads all his mail of course, but that leaves him with a perpetual feeling of guilt he can never quite throw off.

Does your new book spill the beans on the secret relationship between Jesus and Mary Magdalene?

FREKE & GANDY: That's what everyone wants to know about, probably because we've become obsessed with celebrity gossip. If you want the full inside story on their mystical marriage you'll have to read the book, but let's just say that Mary isn't known as Jesus' 'Beloved Disciple' for nothing.

Aren't you worried people will find your new book offensive?

FREKE & GANDY: So far we haven't had any death threats, but we do get lots of 'after-death' threats. Apparently a small corner of Hell has been reserved for us, where we'll be tortured for ever…. by a God of love! Now *that* is a truly offensive idea - don't you think?!

A life size phtograph of Tim Freke

Tim Freke & Peter Gandy

The Gospel of the Second Coming:
Jesus is back... and this time he's funny!

Timothy Freke and Peter Gandy are internationally respected authorities on Christian Gnosticism, whose scholarly books, such as *The Jesus Mysteries*, have been bestsellers throughout the world. In their new book they have put their groundbreaking theories into the form of a satirical Gnostic gospel, which is full of both profound wisdom and edgy humour.

In *The Gospel of the Second Coming* Jesus returns to reveal to the modern world the secrets of the state of enlightenment the original Christians called 'gnosis'. He takes us on a roller coaster of a ride through history, philosophy and mythology, spiced up with a healthy dose of parody.

Here's a little taste of what is sure to be one of the most controversial books of the year...

CHAPTER 1

And so it came to pass that Jesus spoke to the twelve, saying, 'I will reveal to you the mystery of mysteries, which it is my ministry to disclose. The good news that leads to eternal life. The truth that will set you free. Be not afraid when I tell you that I am not who you think I am. I am not a man of flesh and blood. In fact I don't really exist at all. I am the fictional hero of an allegorical myth.'

A great silence fell upon the disciples and Jesus added, 'I know it's a bit of shock.'

Then Peter spoke in amazement, saying, 'Lord, I understand not the wisdom of your words.'

And Jesus replied, 'Listen up and I will reveal the astonishing truth. What I am exists far beyond this world we inhabit. Jesus is a character in a story and I am the Author speaking through Jesus.'

Peter looked gobsmacked, so the Lord explained, 'I am the creator of the story, so I am everything in the story. I am this rock and that piece of wood. Whatever you do to anyone you do to me. Look inside yourself and I am there. Do you get it now?'

'You're saying you're God!' announced Peter enthusiastically. 'I like the sound of that. It's a bit blasphemous, but extremely impressive. And as one of your close disciples, it makes me look good.'

'That's just theological twaddle. I'm trying to tell you something obvious about our predicament right now,' complained Jesus impatiently. 'You and I are characters in a story being imagined by the Author. We don't really exist.'

'Look, Lord, we'll never set up the biggest religious cult in history with this "no one really exists" nonsense,' advised Peter. 'Leave the philosophy to Socrates. Think of your market. Stick with the simple parables and homey homilies. "The Good Samaritan." You know the sort of thing.'

'But we're in a parable right now, for Heaven's sake,' replied Jesus, beginning to find Peter irritating as always. 'This is a fable and we're symbolic figures in it. Understand and be astonished.'

'I'm astonished, all right! I've been going

along with your crazy ideas for a year now, but to be honest I've had enough. One minute you're God. Then you're just a man. Then you don't exist at all. Next you're going to tell me that your water into wine stunt was a cheap conjuring trick done with mirrors.'

'Speculating about how I pulled off my miracles is a complete waste of time, because I didn't really do any miracles!'

'I'm not sure about this new direction, Jesus,' complained Peter. 'I like my heroes to be historical. And I like my miracles to be genuine supernatural anomalies.'

'It's not a new direction, it's just the truth,' insisted Jesus. 'I've always referred to myself as "the Son of Man", which is a Semitic idiom meaning simply "a man"—any man. It's a literary device to show that I'm an Everyman figure in a symbolic myth.'

'Well, you're a lot more than that to me, Lord. As far as I'm concerned, you walk on water. Literally!'

'It's a *metaphor*, for Christ's sake!' said Jesus, unable to contain his exasperation.

Peter felt the anger of the Lord and fell into penitential silence. Finally he said sheepishly, 'I have no idea what you are talking about, Jesus. Sorry.'

'Of course you don't, dear Peter,' said Jesus, adopting a shepherdly tone. 'You represent the foolish person in this story, which is why I gave you the name "Peter", meaning "clod". You play the part of a clod who doesn't really get it, whilst I play the lucid mouthpiece for the wisdom of the Author.'

'That doesn't sound very fair,' muttered Peter, a bit put out.

'Fair or unfair is irrelevant. We don't exist. We're made-up characters in a story.'

'Well, what about Mary?' asked Peter petulantly. 'I suppose she's real enough! You'll look pretty sad if it turns out you've been sleeping with an imaginary woman!'

'Steady on, Peter,' cautioned Jesus. 'You know there's nothing about any of that in the Jesus story. At least not in the official version.'

Then Mary Magdalene spoke, saying, 'Yes, Lord, please do tell. I suppose I don't really exist either? And, as a woman, I find that disappointingly patriarchal.'

And Jesus answered her, saying, 'You are also a character in this great story. You play the part of the foolish soul who is lost in the world, searching for love in all the wrong places. But you are redeemed by the Christ and become the wise soul who listens and understands.'

'I didn't understand a word of that,' declared Mary, because she was usually pretty honest, although she did occasionally tell a few white lies about her past.

'You don't understand *yet*,' Jesus reassured her. 'But you will by the end of this gospel.'

'I'm sure you're right. You're always right,' conceded Mary, because she was on a bit of a guru trip with Jesus and wrongly assumed he was infallible about everything.

'It's only because I am the voice of the Author who has the prerogative of deciding what will turn out to be right,' confessed Jesus.

'So let me get this straight,' said Mary. 'You're saying this is just a story.'

'Bingo!' exclaimed Jesus anachronistically.

'But doesn't that make all our adventures together completely meaningless?' asked Mary. 'It all felt so important when I believed it was real. Now it seems like a bit of a damp squib.'

'The opposite is the truth,' replied Jesus reassuringly. 'Understanding that the Jesus story is a myth reveals its true significance. You see, the Jesus story is an allegory for the spiritual journey each person must make if they are to awaken to the mystical state that the original Christians called "Gnosis", which means "knowledge".'

Then he added portentously, 'And what's more, I am going to decode the allegorical meaning of the Jesus story and reveal the secret teachings of Gnosis later in this gospel. Only this time I'll mix the heavy stuff up with some witty banter to make it more entertaining for the masses.'

'Wow! Secret teachings!' enthused Mary. 'Sounds fantastic!'

'Sounds like flippant nonsense,' complained Peter.

'This gospel will be flippant. But not *just* flippant,' explained Jesus. 'Satire also has a serious side, which is what makes it the highest form of wit. After all, the real literary stars of the ancient world are satirists such as Menippus and Lucian. Their hilarious rants about wandering miracle-workers making a fortune out of the gullible are a hoot. So I've decided to do this new gospel in the same genre. '

And Peter interrupted, saying, 'Exactly how much Eucharist have you been drinking?'

So, realizing he must try harder to stay on topic, Jesus replied, 'I'm sorry. I must try to watch my tendency to indulge in obscure digressions. After all, I screwed it up last time by being too cryptic.'

'Last time?' queried Peter.

'There I go again,' said Jesus cryptically.

Peter looked as confused as Catholic theology, so the Lord comforted him, saying, 'It's of no importance that you understand, Peter. I am not speaking for your benefit, but for the reader who is reading these words. It is the reader I desire to set free. It is the reader to whom I will reveal the secrets of Gnosis.'

'Who the hell is the reader?!' asked Peter.

'A good question,' said Jesus. 'And one I hope the reader will ask themselves, because that question leads to Gnosis.'

Then he added, 'This gospel is going to demand that the reader engage deeply with the ideas I am going to explore. They'll need an open mind, because I am going to suggest that they are also a character in a story.'

'You've gone completely bonkers,' concluded Peter with a disgruntled snort.

And Jesus told him straight, 'It's no good arguing with me. I don't really exist.'

'Do you know your problem, Jesus?' pronounced Peter pointedly. 'You're obsessed by your own non-existence. Just let yourself *be* for a moment.'

Then Peter put his arm around Jesus in a blokey sort of way and suggested amicably, 'Curse a couple of fig trees like you used to do in the old days. You'll feel yourself again in no time.'

And so it came to pass that the Lord pulled himself up straight, because normally he had a bit of a hunch like the Dalai Lama, and bellowed, 'You're as brainless as a rock! If I'm not careful, you'll go off and found an authoritarian church based on a complete misunderstanding of my teachings, which will inhibit humanity's spiritual evolution for nearly two millennia.'

Then he added, 'That's why I agreed to do this *Gospel of the Second Coming* and clear things up once and for all.'

Jesse Folks

The Gospel of Judas

Upon publication in 2006, the *Gospel of Judas* immediately sparked a media tempest. A rough transcription of the Coptic text, along with a basic translation by a team of scholars assembled by National Geographic, was released in conjunction with a handful of books on the gospel and one television documentary. These initial studies claimed that the gospel treated the character of Judas very positively, even redeeming him as the most enlightened apostle and an exemplary Gnostic. Since then, however, several scholars have questioned this conclusion, citing instances in the Coptic text where the National Geographic translators made a range of errors, which included omitting negatives and translating certain Coptic-Greek words using outdated classical senses rather than the senses they had in Christian Egypt. A very accessible summary of these problems is April D. DeConick's *The Thirteenth Apostle*, which addresses each issue in detail. She is the Isla Carroll and Percy E. Turner Professor of Biblical Studies in the Department of Religious Studies at Rice University in Houston, Texas.

What is this enigmatic gospel that has gone from obscurity to global fame? In his famous anti-Gnostic polemic *Against Heresies*, the second-century saint Irenaeus of Lyons talks about a group of so-called Gnostics whom he calls Cainites. They supposedly composed a *Gospel of Judas* in which the commonly loathed apostle was taught the mysteries of the universe by his master, Jesus. In the 1970s near Al Minya, Egypt, a leather-bound codex was discovered that contained four Coptic Gnostic texts, including a *Gospel of Judas*. It was designated Codex Tchacos after the collector who gave

the to scholars for study. If the *Gospel of Judas* found in the 1970s is the same *Gospel of Judas* known to Irenaeus, the original Greek version must predate Irenaeus' *Against Heresies,* written around 180 CE. The Coptic copy in Codex Tchacos was likely produced around the same time as the Nag Hammadi Library, sometime during the fourth century CE. It is not known when this text was initially translated from the original Greek into Coptic.

The *Gospel of Judas* is an example of a form of ancient Judeo-Christian Gnosticism called 'Sethianism' that flourished from the second through fourth centuries of the Common Era. This was an originally Egyptian and Syrian form of Gnostic thought that considered the God of the Old Testament to be a devilish impostor for the One True God. It held that Adam's third son Seth was the progenitor of a race of enlightened spirituals, of which the Sethian Gnostics were heirs.

The *Gospel of Judas* raises some questions for the person interested in early Christian history as well as the spiritual seeker. It is an interesting coincidence that the text resurfaced just recently, as interest in early Christianity is on the rise and more and more modern Christians are asking the same difficult questions about evil that the ancient Gnostics asked – for instance, why does the God of the Old Testament sometimes act in ways we might consider contrary to the God described by Jesus in the New Testament? It is tempting to try and take the text as a history – a literal account of events that might have happened in the presence of Jesus. The reader must be careful to understand that the text is essentially a pious fiction. It is a take on Judas that addresses questions that might have weighed heavily on the ancient Christian mind.

The author shows Jesus as critical of thanksgiving rituals that resemble a primitive Eucharist, a ritual which the proto-Orthodox (the Christian party that would eventually become the orthodox church of Nicea in 325) as well as numerous early Christian sects, some Gnostics themselves, regularly practiced. The Eucharist is portrayed as a ritual based on bloody sacrifice, and though Jesus is not yet handed over in the world of the narrative itself, the text gives the feeling that the author viewed the crucifixion as a tragedy rather than a passion play.

The author is also very critical of the Apostles, who are portrayed as knowing very little and understanding even less. As in the *Gospel of Mark,* the Apostles just don't get it. Many Christian sects – both orthodox and heterodox – based their authority on teachings transmitted by these same characters of whom the *Gospel of Judas* is so critical. The text implicitly raises the question of spiritual authority. Does it come from a line of transmission, as the apostolic churches claimed? Or does it come from individual experience of the 'mysteries of the Kingdom?' While the *Gospel of Judas'* response to the first question is decidedly negative, the answer to the second is more difficult.

Perhaps the most provocative point in the *Gospel of Judas* is how it treats the Gnostic idea of salvation by Gnosis. In the text, Jesus teaches Judas the mysteries of the kingdom, 'Not so that you will go there yourself, but that you will grieve all the more when another replaces you.' Judas is clearly the most enlightened of the bunch, and is even able to stand under Jesus' gaze (though he cannot look Jesus in the eyes). It seems that as far as his spiritual maturity and acquaintance with the mysteries goes, Judas is advanced beyond the abilities of his fellow Apostles. Strangely, Gnosis does not seem to be enough for Judas! Judas is still condemned as the 'thirteenth demon' and told he will not enter the house of the saints that he saw in his vision, because he will exceed the evil deeds of all the others and 'sacrifice the man

who bears' Jesus.

For scholars, this is quite a conundrum. Is this text deviant from the rest of the Sethian corpus in asserting that Gnosis can, in at least Judas' case, count for little? Or is this a clue into an overlooked aspect of Sethianism? Might this be evidence of a rigid Gnostic determinism where your spiritual destiny is unavoidable no matter what insight you achieve? It is problematic for scholars, but the real burden falls on the modern spiritual seeker who wishes to find the pearls in the mud of this confusing and fragmentary ancient work. It is difficult to answer any of these questions for sure. If Gnosis is not enough for Judas, what else would he have needed to do to establish himself in the plan of salvation?

I had the opportunity to go over this text in exhaustive detail in a graduate Coptic class this semester, and ultimately we came to a conclusion similar to that of Dr. DeConick. Judas is not a positive character in the *Gospel of Judas,* but a traitor of demonic nature whose betrayal of Jesus would ultimately promote him to the rank and stature of the hated Sethian Demiurge, Yaldabaoth. The following translation reflects these developments, which are explained in the footnotes. A full consensus of scholars regarding how to interpret this Gospel is still some years away, but the general lines of thought outlined here seem to be reasonably well established.

The secret verdict[1] which Jesus discussed with Judas during the week, three days before he celebrated Passover.

When Jesus appeared on earth he performed signs and great wonders for mankind's salvation. Indeed, some did walk the path of righteousness, but others walked in their transgression. The twelve disciples were called. He began to discuss with them the mysteries of the universe[2] and the events that would transpire. A number of times he did not reveal himself to his disciples, but you might find him in their midst as an apparition.[3]

He was in Judea with his disciples one day and he found them sitting together practicing piety. When he approached his disciples seated together saying grace over bread,[4] he laughed. The disciples said to him, 'Master, why do you laugh at our giving thanks? Haven't we done what is right?' He answered and said to them, 'I'm not laughing at you. You're not doing this by your own will but so that your god

1

Van der Vliet points out that the word 'apophasis,' a Greek word being used by the Coptic translator or transcriber of the MS, is more related to a verdict or sentence than Meyer's translation as 'declaration.' The Greek word αποφασις does appear to mean something neutral to negative (Liddell and Scott 9th ed, 226a). It is a judgment, or sentence. If the transcriber or translator merely brought the word over from the Greek (a common practice among Coptic transcribers), it is unlikely that this word is translatable with a word with such positive religious connotations as 'revelation.' (Van der Vliet, 140).

2

Κοσμος. This word has a variety of meanings from 'household order' to 'the system' to 'the universe.' (Liddell and Scott 983a)

3

Meyer translates N̄2PO̅T 'a child,' from the Bohairic ḫРОϯ (Crum 631 a-b). He suggests however that it may also be the Bohairic/Sahidic 2OРТ/ϢOРТ (Crum 588b). I feel that the context of the sentence suggests the second reading, 'apparition.'

4

'They were giving thanks' is the proper verbal translation of ⲈⲨⲢ ⲈⲨⲬⲀⲢⲒⲤⲦⲒ. Though it might be tempting to interpret this passage as a reference to the Eucharist, the Greek word that the Coptic derives from, ευχαριστεω, is a common word both Hellenistic and Judaic cultures to mean the simple act of 'saying grace' or 'giving thanks.' The author(s) might have intended either meaning (grace or Eucharist), or perhaps both. Considering the time setting of the narrative, rather than the document's composition, I have chosen 'saying grace.'

may be blessed. They said, 'Master, aren't you the son of our god?' Jesus said to them, 'How do you know me? Amen I say to you, no human generation will know me among any of you.'

But when the disciples heard this they were vexed, enraged even, and blasphemed him in their hearts. When Jesus saw their ignorance, he said to them, 'Why all the angry frustration? Your god who is in you and his [servants] have frustrated your souls. May the one who is solid among men from among you bring out the perfect person and stand before my face.' They all said 'We're strong enough!' but none of their spirits were strong enough to stand before his face, save Judas. He was able to stand, but he couldn't look Jesus in the eyes, and turned his face away.[5] Judas said to him, 'I know who you are and where you come from. You have come from the immortal Aeon Barbelo. He who sent you, His name I am unworthy to pronounce.'[6] But Jesus, knowing he was thinking about lofty things, said to him, 'Come away from them. I will tell you the mysteries of the Kingdom, not so that you will go there yourself, but that you will grieve all the more when another replaces you so that the twelve disciples might be complete before their god.' Judas said to him, 'Can you tell me when these things happen? When the great day of light dawns for the [?][7]

5

The Coptic ⲘⲠⲈⲘⲦⲞ ⲈⲂⲞⲖ ⲘⲠⲀⲠⲢⲞⲤⲞⲠⲞⲚ means 'before my face.' Judas cannot look Jesus in the eyes, and turns his head. This might suggest that Judas is more spiritually advanced than the other disciples, but to negative ends that would make Judas ashamed.

6

April DeConick believes much of this narrative to parody canonical traditions, most specifically Mark. In the world of the Gospel narratives, most regular people are portrayed as having little clue to Jesus' true nature or mission. The characters who consistently recognize Jesus' divine nature on sight, however, are demons (see Mark 1:34, 3:11, 5:6-7). In the context of Mark, Judas' recognition of Christ for who he truly is and his apparently unexpected knowledge of 'lofty things' like the Aeon Barbelo might betray a demonic nature of some sort working through or within Judas (DeConick 106-108).

7

Human? Perfect? Holy? The papyrus is unreadable. In this translation, indeterminate text is shown with a bracketed question mark. Where conjecture is reasonable, the conjectural text is in brackets. Any bracketed text is theoretical – more accurate conjecture would require a careful reconstruction of the missing Coptic text.

generation?' But when he said these things, Jesus left him.

He appeared to his disciples early and they said to him, 'Master! Where did you go? What did you do when you left us?' Jesus told them, 'I went to another great and holy generation.' The disciples said to him, 'Lord, what is this great generation that is so much loftier and holier than us and isn't even in these aeons?' Suddenly, when Jesus heard this, he laughed. He said to them, 'Why do you contemplate the strong and holy generation? Amen I say to you, no one born of this aeon will see that generation, nor will any host of angels from the stars lord over it. Nor will anyone born of mortals attain to it. That generation is not from [that aeon] which is [the abode of the saints] but the generation of men among you is from the human generation [?] power [?] by which you rule.'

When the disciples heard this their spirits were disturbed. Not one could find anything to say.

When Jesus came to them another day, they said to him, 'Master, we saw you in a vision! Great dreams dawned on us last night that were all alike.' He said, 'Why have you [gone] and hidden yourselves?' So they said, 'We saw a great house, a great altar inside it, and 12 men (whom we say are priests). And a name. There was a crowd offering devotions at the sacrificial altar there. When the priests finished they took the offering. We were also giving our own devotions.' Jesus said, 'In what manner [are they sacrificing]?' They said, 'Indeed, some fast for two weeks, but others are sacrificing their own children, others their wives, in blessings and pieties for one another! Some sleep with males, others do destructive deeds. Even more commit a plethora of sins and unruly deeds, and the men stand upon the altar and call *your* name! While they're involved with the particulars of the sacrifice, the altar is filled up.' After they said this, they were quiet and disturbed.

Jesus asked them, 'Why are you disturbed? All the priests who stand before that altar call upon my name. I say to you, my name was written on [the book] of the generation of the stars by the generation of men, and they shamefully planted fruitless trees in my name.' He continued, 'You are those who worship at the altar which you saw. That one is the god whom you serve, and the twelve you saw are yourselves. The cattle you saw brought in are the sacrifices, the many whom you mislead upon that altar. The [?] will stand this is how he will use my name, and the pious generations will be devoted to him. After him another man will stand up from among the fornicators, and another from the child killers, and another from the man-lovers and those who fast, and the rest of the unclean and the lawless and the erroneous, and those who say, "We are like angels."[8] They are the stars that bring all to completion. For it was told to the human generations, "Behold, God receives your sacrifice from the hand of a priest," who is a minister of error. But the Lord, who is Lord over the All, commands that they shall be convicted on the last day.'

[The bottom half of a papyrus sheet is missing (pages 41 and 42 of the MS), preserving only the top 8 lines. Just three lines are readable in a photographic fragment of page 41 that the MS editors think might have belonged to this leaf]

Jesus said to them, 'Stop sacrificing! What you [place] upon the altar are above your stars and your angels have already reached their end there. So let them [be]. Before you, they go [to their own ends].

...to the generations. A baker is unable to feed all creation under heaven.' [They were confused.] They said to him, '[Explain this] to us and [we may understand].' Jesus said to them, 'Stop struggling with

---

8

 Perhaps this last group criticized is the Valentinians, who believed themselves to be the material counterpart to a spiritual angelic twin. Perhaps it is a direct reference to Luke 20:36, where people worthy of the resurrection are celibate and thus 'equal to the angels.' Perhaps it is simply a reference to another Christian group or author making use of this passage.

me. You each have your own star there,[9] and everyone [is bound by fate].'

…in the [?] and where he did not go which [?] the spring of the tree [?] of this aeon. After a time, he came to water God's paradise, and the generation will remain, in order to not pollute that generation's conduct. But this generation has it forever and ever.' Judas said to him, 'Rabbi, what is the fruit of this generation?' Jesus said, 'Every soul among human generations will die, but when these complete the time of the kingdom and the spirit leaves them, their bodies die, but their souls will be quickened and taken up.' Judas said, 'What will the other generations of men do?' Jesus said, 'It is an impossible task to sow on a rock and receive fruit. So then, this is the way [of] the defiled race of corrupt Sophia, the hand that created mortal people, and their souls go up to the aeons above. Amen I say to you, neither ruler nor angel nor power can see that place that this great and holy generation will see.' When Jesus said this, he left.

Judas said, 'Master, as you've listened to all this, listen to me also, for I saw a great vision.' When Jesus heard this, he laughed and said to him, 'Why do you strive so, oh thirteenth demon?[10] But say your piece, I am bearing with you.' Judas said to him, 'In the vision I saw myself, and the 12 disciples were throwing stones at me and persecuting me greatly. Again I came to the place [where they waited] behind you. I saw a house and my eyes were unable to comprehend its size. Great people surrounded it, and it had one single[11] roof. And in the middle

---

9

Considering that the author portrays Jesus as associating the disciples with the 12 archonic rulers of the zodiac, assigning them each a star is not a positive gesture but shows they are under the power of the archons and fate.

10

ⲆⲀⲒⲘⲞⲚ – means 'demon,' an evil spirit, in general Coptic Christian usage. (DeConick, 48-51). Several translators have translated this word as the more neutral term 'spirit,' but this use is anachronistic to the Christian usage during the time the Coptic *Gospel of Judas* was translated.

of the house was a crowd.' [Judas said,] 'Master, take me also inside with these people.' Jesus answered and said, 'Your star has mislead you, Judas.' And he said, 'No mortal can enter the house you saw, for that's the place reserved for the saints, the place where neither sun nor moon will rule, nor the day. They will stand there always in the aeon with the holy angels. Behold, I have told you the mysteries of the kingdom, and I have taught you about the error of the stars and [about] the 12 aeons.'

Judas said, 'Master, surely my seed is not under the authority of the archons!' Jesus said to him, 'Come and I will [show you] but you will lament greatly when you see the kingdom and its entire generation.' When Judas heard this he said to him, 'What good is this to me since you've separated me from that generation?'[12] Jesus answered and said, 'You will become the thirteenth, and will be cursed by all the remaining generations. You will rule over them. In the last days they will [?] you. You are not going[13] to the heights, to the holy generation.'

Jesus said, 'Come, so I might teach you about [things] which no person can see. For there is a great and boundless aeon. No generation of angels sees its magnitude, and the great invisible Spirit is within it. This is the one whom no angel's eye has seen, nor a thought of a heart has received, nor is it called by any name. A shiny cloud appeared in that place there and it said, "Let an angel be my help." A great angel,

11
ОҮСТЄГН NOYOTЄ – The second word here is unattested anywhere else. Meyer translates 'a roof of greenery.' He suggests that it could also be read as a misspelling of ОҮОСТN, so 'a broad roof.' I think it is an alternate spelling of the Sahidic ОҮⲰTЄ, or 'single' (Crum 494a; Van der Vliet, 145).

12
This sentence is difficult. It is something like, 'What is the greater which I have received since you have separated from that generation?' ⲀКΠОРⲬT ЄTГЄNЄⲀ ЄTMMⲀҮ is 'you separated me from that generation' (Crum 271b-272a).

1   3
'not going' – NЄКBⲰК is a 3rd future negative in Lycopolitan, a minority dialect in this text. It carries a prophetic connotation in this context.

Autogenes,[14] god of light, came out of the cloud. Because of him, there were four other angels in another cloud, and they were servants for the angelic Autogenes, god of light. The four other angels from another cloud existed because of him. They became a help to the angelic Autogenes. Then Autogenes said, "Let Adamas exist!" The emanation happened and he created the first luminary to rule over him. He said, "Let there be angels worshipping him," and a numberless throng came into being. He said, "Let there be an aeon of light," and so there was. He created a second luminary to rule over him with the numberless throng of angels worshipping. That is how he created the rest of the aeons of light, and he made them to rule over them. He created for them numberless throngs of angels who assist them. Adamas was in the first cloud. This was the light which no angel could see among all those called "divine." And he [?] that [?] the image [?] and according to the likeness of this angel. He revealed the incorruptible generation of Seth. The twelve [?]. The twenty-four [?]. By the will of the Spirit, he manifested 72 luminaries in the incorruptible generation. The 72 manifested 360 luminaries, or 5 luminaries each. The Father is the 12 aeons and twelve luminaries, 6 heavens per aeon so that there might be 72 heavens for 72 luminaries and 5 firmaments[15] for each of them so that there might be 360 firmaments. Power was given to them, and a great host of angels, numberless, for their glory and worship. Virgin spirits, too, for glorifying and worshiping of all the aeons and the heavens and their firmaments. The Father, his 72 luminaries, the Autogenes, and his 72 aeons call that crowd of immortals "Universe,"[16] which is death.[17] The first human appeared there with his incorruptible powers.

1   4
'Self-Generated.'

15
"'Firmament' is a difficult word to translate. There just isn't a modern concept similar enough. It is the ancient idea that the sky is a big dome.

16
Κοσμος. The virgin spirits are the Kosmos? Or all the immortals listed in the revelation? It is confusing to me exactly who the author intends to be included in 'that crowd of immortals.'

17
Φθορα (Liddell and Scott 1930 a&b). This is not a nice word. At best, it is a word to describe shipwrecks,

But the aeon who appeared with his generation, the one who contains the cloud of gnosis[18] and the angel, is called [?] El [?] and aeon [?] and afterwards Autogenes said, "Let there be twelve angels, ruling over Chaos and Hell[19]." And behold, an angel appeared from the cloud whose face poured fourth fire, its likeness dirty with blood, named Nebro, which means Apostate, but yet others call him Yaldabaoth. Another angel came out of the cloud, Saklas. Nebro created 6 angels and Saklas for help and these produced 12 angels in heaven and each took a part of heaven. The 12 archons spoke with the 12 angels, "Let each of you [serve us]." And they [served them]. [The] five angels [did likewise]. The first is [?]who is called the Christ. The second is Harmathoth, who [?][20]. The third is Galila. The fourth is Yobel, the fith Adonaios. Those are the five who rule over Hell, and the principals of Chaos. Then Saklas said to his angels, "Let us create a man according to our likeness and image." So they formed Adam and his wife Eve (but in the cloud she was called Life, and by this name all the generations seek after it, and each calls her by their names for her). But Sakla didn't [?]. And the archon said to him, "Your life will be [brief]. [Spend your] time with your children."'

Judas said to Jesus, 'How long does a person live?' Jesus said, 'Why do you want to know? Adam and his generation received his time such

and at worst, total annihilation. Its meanings range from ruin, destruction, and mayhem to death and oblivion.

18
Γνωσις. (Liddell and Scott 355a)

19
The word here is ⲀⲘⲈⲚⲦⲈ, literally 'the west.' In Egyptian culture the west of the Nile was a common burial ground and so 'The West' became an epithet for the underworld. In Christian usage, this term became decidedly negative, and took on the connotation of 'Hell.'

20
Seth? Atheth? Meyer's translation reads 'Seth, who is called "the Christ." ' DeConick suggests that the sentence reads 'Atheth, who is called "the good one," ' interpreting 'Atheth' as an alternate spelling for the Sethian archon 'Athoth' and the X̄C̄ nomina sacra as meaning ⲬⲢⲈⲤⲦⲞⳫ (Chrestos, 'the good one'), rather than the common ⲬⲢⲓⲤⲦⲞⳫ (Christos, 'Christ'). Chrestos was a common moniker for the archon Athoth in Sethian literature. (DeConick, 85; Also see the following post on her website: http://forbiddengospels. blogspot.com/2008/02/answering-tonys-questions-about.html)

a period there and he received his kingdom and his archon.'

Judas said to Jesus, 'Does the human spirit die?' Jesus said, 'This is how God ordered Michael to endow human spirits: as a loan, so that they might return them.[21] But it is the Great One who ordered Gabriel to endow the spirits of the great kingless generation, both spirit and soul. Therefore these remaining souls…[?] them [?] light [?] surrounding [?] Spirit in you [?] which make you dwell in this body in the angelic generation. God let them give gnosis[22] to Adam and his company so that the kings of Chaos and of Hell might not rule over them.' So Judas said to Jesus, 'What will those generations do, then?' Jesus said, 'Truly I say to you, the stars are coming to completion over all things, but when Saklas completes his time which has been fixed for him, their first star will come with the generations and what they have said. They too will come to completion. Then they will fornicate in my name and slay their children…[?] and they will [?] and they will…

[5 lines missing]

…in my name, and your star will rule over the Thirteenth Aeon.'

Afterwards, Jesus laughed, and Judas said, 'Master, why do you laugh at us?' Jesus answered and said, 'I'm not laughing at you but at the error of the stars, because these 6 stars wander around with these 5 warriors and all those will be destroyed with their creatures.'

Judas said to Jesus, 'What will the baptized do in your name?' Jesus

---

21
  Literally, 'serving the loan,' or repaying the loan obligation.

22
22 Γνωσις (Liddell and Scott 355a)

said, "Truly I say to you, this baptism in my name... [?]

[5 lines missing]

to me...[?] 'Truly I say to you, Judas, those who sacrifice to Saklas [blaspheme] God.'

[3 incomplete lines]

...everything evil. But you, you will exceed them all, for you will sacrifice the man who bears me. Already your horn has been raised, and your wrath is full, and your star passes by, and your heart is determined. Truly I say to you, your last...[?] become [?] is [?] grieving. [?] ...the archon, having been obliterated. Then the type of the great generation of Adam will be exalted, for that generation, which is before the sky, the earth, and the angels, exists through the aeons. Behold, everything has been told to you. Lift your eyes and see the cloud and the light within and the stars surrounding it. The star which is leading, that is your star." So Judas lifted his eyes up and saw the luminous cloud. He[23] went inside it. Those standing below heard a voice sounding from the cloud, saying, 'The great generation... [8 lines damaged]

The high priests murmured because he went to the guest room and prayed. But some of the scribes there were watching, so they might arrest him during the prayer, but they feared him because the crowd considered him to be a prophet for them all. They approached Judas and said to him, 'What are you doing here? You're Jesus' disciple!' So he answered them as they wished.[24] Judas took the money and handed him over to them.

23
'He.' Judas? Jesus? The antecedent is not completely clear.
24
Were they expecting him? To what does this refer?

Bibliography and Further Reading

Crum, Walter E. *A Coptic Dictionary*. Oxford: Clarendon, 1939.
    The authoritative Coptic dictionary.

DeConick, April. *The Thirteenth Apostle: What the Gospel of Judas Really Says*. New York: Continuum, 2007.
    DeConick's groundbreaking book on the translation issues of this fascinating text and a discussion on how the author evaluates Judas' character.

Kasser, Rodolphe and Gregor Wurst. *The Gospel of Judas: Critical Edition*. Washington DC: National Geographic, 2007.
    The recent critical edition of the Gospel of Judas, with Coptic text, English and French translations by Marvin Meyer and Rodolphe Kasser, and facsimile photos of each leaf and fragment of papyrus in the codex.

Layton, Bentley. *A Coptic Grammar: Sahidic Dialect*. Wiesbaden: Harrassowitz Verlag, 2000.
    A technical but authoritative handbook on the particulars of Coptic Grammar.

Liddell and Scott. *Greek-English Lexicon, 9th Edition*. Oxford, 1996.
    The authoritative resource on Greek vocabulary.

Smith, Richard H. *A Concise Coptic-English Lexicon*. 2nd rev. ed. Atlanta: Scholars Press, 1999.
    An inexpensive and easy to use Coptic lexicon.

Van der Vliet, Jacques. 'Judas and the Stars', *The Journal of Juristic Papyrology*, 36 (2006) pp.137-152.
    An article discussing several issues in the *Gospel of Judas*, including astrological themes and some important translation issues.

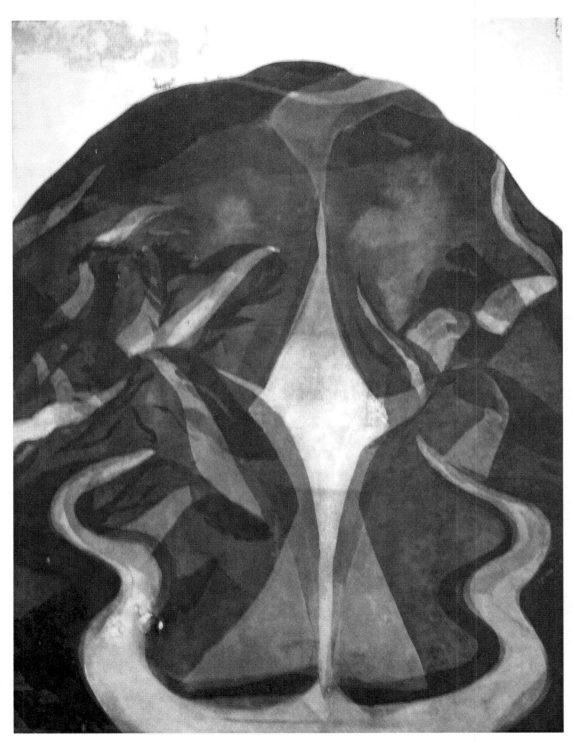

Mount Carmel by Scott D. Finch

Andrew Phillip Smith

The Alternative Judas

In Christianity, Peter's mere denial of Jesus may be considered to be a very human failing which is redeemed by Peter's subsequent rocklike devotion to Christ. But Judas' betrayal was irredeemable, he was the arch-traitor, the embodiment of unatonable evil. Dante placed him in the lowest circle of Hell, right next to his pal Satan.

The *Gospel of Judas*, rediscovered only in the last quarter of the twentieth century and published in 2006, brought the received view of Judas back into question. Was Judas perhaps the favoured disciple of Jesus, privy to his most secret teaching? When, in the *Gospel of Judas*, he handed Jesus over to the Jews, was he perhaps performing his required duty, just doing his job? Judas' brief redemption in the public consciousness has been challenged by subsequent scholarship which argues that Judas the hero was merely the result of over-hasty publication by the closed circle of scholars required by the commercial demands of National Geographic, the licensed publishers of the Codex Tchacos manuscript.

So, is he or isn't he? Is the Judas of The *Gospel of Judas* a Gnostic hero, the one disciple picked out by Jesus to receive his secret teaching, who then selflessly took on the part of betraying Jesus so that his master would be crucified and thus the divine mission would be accomplished? Or was he simply the most typical of the twelve apostles, all of whom worshipped the demiurge instead of the true God, Judas merely being the one who actually sacrificed Jesus to the demiurge? The initial translation and interpretation by the National Geographic team plumped for

the former option; the new translation by Jesse Folks featured in this issue follows the Coptic rigorously, with the benefit of subsequent scholarship, and concludes that Judas is 'a traitor of demonic nature whose betrayal of Jesus will ultimately promote him to the rank and stature of the hated Sethian Demiurge, Yaldabaoth.'

Was there ever an alternative view of Judas, one which sees him as other than the infamous traitor and betrayer? If we step aside from interpretative issues in the *Gospel of Judas* for a moment, we can discover a variety of interpretations of Judas throughout the history of Christianity. If the newly-discovered *Gospel of Judas* merely depicts Judas as being the same type of villain as the other apostles, we still have the description of a *Gospel of Judas* by the second-century church father Irenaeus, which, whether Irenaus' account is based on another *Gospel of Judas* or on a misinterpretation of our *Gospel of Judas*, seems to be hard evidence of a positive attitude towards Judas.

A brief glance over the sea of interpretations available to us will show us that there have always been alternative Judases. Some of these alternative interpretations are bizarre, some profound, but most no more heroic than the Christian account taught at Sunday school.

There have also been scores of modern reinterpretations of Judas, from G.I. Gurdjieff's straightforward declaration that Judas was the greatest disciple of Jesus, fulfilling the role of betrayer in order to buy Jesus the time that he needed to complete his mission to Kazantzakis' portrayal of Judas as Jesus' conscience in *The Last Temptation of Christ*. Surely the most popular fictional account of Judas is the *The Gospel According to Judas; by Benjamin Iscariot* by Conservative-Party-millionaire-jailbird-author Jeffrey Archer, which often gets misplaced in the non-fiction section of bookshops, presumably persuading the bemused customer that Archer's book is the genuine Gnostic gospel. But in this essay I will focus mainly on the interpretations of Judas that were formed in the context of the Abrahamic religions.

In many traditional Christian stories about Judas, he retains his role as traitor, but fascinating details are added. The apocryphal infancy gospels add material related to Jesus' childhood and family background. The author of the *Arabic Infancy Gospel* (which, despite its language of survival, was a Christian not a Muslim work) couldn't resist inserting Judas into his creative retelling of Jesus' early years. According to the *Arabic Infancy Gospel*, Judas' mother was living in the same town as Jesus' family. Judas was 'tormented by Satan' and used continually to bite all those around him—if no one else was available, he would gnaw at his own hands, legs and arms. Once, when sitting next to the boy Jesus, he couldn't resist trying to bite him, but found himself unable to. Instead, as a second best, he struck Jesus on the right side, causing Jesus to weep, in reaction to which Satan, repulsed by the divine tears, fled from Judas in the shape of a dog. This blow to the side of Jesus was a prefiguration of the spear which entered Jesus on the cross, in exactly the same place as Judas' blow.

There are traces of lost dialogues between Jesus and Judas (the Judas in the *Dialogue of the Saviour* is widely believed to be, contra Marvin Meyer in his *Gospels of Judas*, Judas Thomas, who is the apostle Thomas and the same figure as that in the *Gospel of Thomas* and the *Book of Thomas*.) The early second-century church father Papias included a dialogue in his collection of Jesus sayings (which has only been preserved in quotation by Eusebius) which describes a time of apocalypse in which all manner of vegetation— vine clusters, grain, seeds, herbs and fruit will grow in abundance, each begging to be taken by the Lord. Judas is here a rationalistic voice who doubts the veracity of the parable and asks how all of this would be brought about. Jesus cryptically answers that those who will be alive at that time will see it—possibly a reference to Judas' early death. In another excerpt preserved by the heresiologist Hippolytus, Judas asks a similar question in response to Jesus' description of the coming kingdom of the Holy, and is told by Jesus that those who are worthy will see these things—and, sorry Judas, you're not going to be one of them.

Nobody seemed to be certain of the final fate of Judas. The gospels of Mark and John are silent on it, yet we still have three differing accounts of the death of Judas. It is Matthew who gives us the first tale of a post-betrayal Judas. Matthew's brief addendum to the betrayal story (Matt 27:3-10) tells us that Judas realised what he had done and tried to return the thirty pieces to the priests. When they refused, Judas flung back the money in the Temple and hung himself in fulfilment of the scripture (cited as Jeremiah in Matthew but thought by most scholars to be a reference to Zechariah instead.) The priests buy the Potter's Field with the money as a place to bury strangers.

This also features in Luke's version, in Acts 1:16-20, where it is known as the Field of Blood, but Judas was said to have bought it himself with his payoff. Luke maintained that Judas fell headlong and his intestines spilled out. Acts says nothing about hanging and isn't explicit as to whether Judas' death was suicide or misadventure. Over the centuries, many Christians have given in to the temptation of harmonising these two accounts and came up with the inventive solution that Judas' bowels must have spilled out as a result of his hanging (and whose wouldn't?) But Papias gives us an altogether different and equally ghastly tale of Judas' end: He grew fat. So fat that neither his head nor body could fit through an alleyway wide enough for a wagon. He developed cataracts (perhaps Judas was a diabetic?), his genitals grew large and he gave out pus and worms and eventually died on his own land.

In some versions of the apocryphal *Gospel of Nicodemus* or *Acts of Pilate*, Judas goes back home after a hard night's betrayal to find his wife spit-roasting a chicken over their fire. Mrs Iscariot calms Judas, assuring him that Jesus can no more rise from the dead than the roast chicken could crow. Sure enough, the roast chicken flaps its wings and crows three times, in response to which, Judas hangs himself. (Perhaps Peter heard the crowing of the same roast chicken just as he was denying Jesus.)

Even the recruitment of Judas was open to question. The author of the *Gospel of the Ebionites*, an ascetic Jewish-Christian gospels— thought that Judas was one of the seven disciples recruited by Jesus on the shores of Lake Tiberius. Then there was the controversy of the last supper. In John 13:26 Jesus dipped a morsel of bread in oil and gave it to Judas. But the Last Supper was the first Eucharist and so the bread was Jesus' body and the wine his blood. So did Judas receive the body and blood of Christ, and thus the Eucharist? For if Judas was an unrepentant sinner and Jesus knew this then why did Jesus minister the Eucharist to him? And if Judas received the sacrament, how he could have gone on to betray Jesus immediately afterwards? A body of Christian theology, summarised comprehensively by Thomas Aquinas, grew up to discuss this tricky issue. Among the contributors were Augustine, Dionysius, Hilary, and John of Damascus. Careful exegesis of the relevant passages led the church fathers to decide that Judas did not in fact receive the sacrament. (Perhaps he spat it out just after he left the last supper.)

The Manichaean Judas, at least in the Manichaean Crucifixion Hymn, has much the same outline as the Christian version, but a fascinating detail is added: Judas kissed Jesus on the hand as a sign to the night watchman.

A translation (from a French translation) of an Armenian version of the Jesus-Abgar letters contains an interesting take on Judas' blood money.

Jesus said to his disciples: 'Do you know where this money that Abgar sent us as a gift comes from?' And they said: 'We do not know.' And Jesus said: 'The father of Abraham, Thara, made this money and with this money he bought the cave with the son of Amor. The Edessenians took the money and bought Joseph from his brothers. And the brothers of Joseph brought it as a gift to Joseph in Egypt. The Egyptians brought it as a gift to King Solomon, and King Solomon made the door of the Temple with it. When Nebuchadnezar deported Jerusalem, he broke the door and carried it to Babylon. The Babylonians gave it to the Chaldeans. The Chaldeans gave it to the merchants, and the merchants gave it to the shepherds. And Abgar, having received it from the shepherds gave it to us. Now, take this money and carry it to the priests and say: 'Jesus the Nazarean sent it to you.' And the priests, having taken the money, gave it to venal Judas, for which he handed over Christ. And Judas turned over the money and hung himself. And the priests gave it to the soldiers who guarded the tomb of Christ. And they gave it back to the priests and the priests said: 'This money should not be kept, because it is the price of blood.' Then they gave the money and bought the potter's field and made it a cemetery for foreigners.[1]

This midrash on the thirty pieces of silver, following the trail of money through various biblical episodes, has some similarity to the treatment of the legend of the cross in *The Golden Legend*, an astonishingly popular medieval collection of saints' lives that includes reworkings of the cycle of stories surrounding the life of Jesus, in which the piece of wood that is eventually made into the cross has a similarly long history of involvement with biblical events. Initially, Adam's son Seth took a branch from the tree of life and planted it on Adam's tomb, strangely suggestive of Sethian Gnostic influence.[2]

A surprising but persistent development

involves the recasting of Judas in an oedipal role. Did Judas make the beast with two backs with his ma and do away with his pa? Medieval Christians thought so. It was Origen who first compared Judas and Oedipus, his aim being to convince his pagan opponent Celsus that, like Oedipus, Judas' betrayal could have been prefigured in scripture without necessitating a denial of the principle of free will.

In the *Golden Legend*, the Oedipal interpretation reached its full development. Judas is here the son of two Jews, Reuben and Cyborea. After Judas is conceived, Cyborera has a dream that their son will be so evil that the Jewish people will be destroyed. They abandon him, but he has an identifying mark, either a birthmark or a mutilation given to him by his parents. He is placed in a basket and abandoned to the waters, but the basket shores up on the island of Iskariot (whence Judas' surname) and Judas is brought up by the king and queen. They also have a son of their own, whom Judas kills once he discovers that he is adopted. Judas flees and ends up in the service of Herod (or in some versions, Pontius Pilate) who sends Judas to steal fruit from Reuben's orchard. Judas is caught by his father, but kills him and is given Reuben's widow, Judas' mother Cyborea as a wife. Judas repents when he meets Jesus, and the rest of the tale proceeds in a more-or-less canonical fashion. Thus Judas is the victim of fate, yet can demonstrate free will in his repentance and betrayal.

Origen also came up with a complex theological redefining of the Judas story. In Origen's version, God chose Judas because he already had evil in his soul, and God himself directed Judas to the demons. Satan took advantage of this and used Judas to betray Jesus. Jesus' blood was then accepted as a ransom (which is the basis of the concept of redemption) and Satan handed over dead sinners to God in return. The ransom mirrors the thirty pieces of silver accepted by Judas. But in a very Gnostic touch, Jesus' spirit was too strong to be destroyed along with his body and it rose from the dead. Origen spent quite some space detailing Judas'

misgivings over the deed—for instance, Judas' conscience would not allow him to betray Jesus in public and he recognised the enormity of his action to the extent that he returned the thirty pieces of silver and hanged himself. All of this was considered to be the result of Jesus' teaching which lingered on in the soul of Judas. Thus Judas was not wholly bad and, like Job, his trial was at least partly the result of dealings between God and Satan.

Did Judas have descendants? The people of Corfu believed that among the Jews of their island were descendents of the traitor, and that Judas' house and country retreat had been on their island. On Easter Eve they threw crockery onto the street in a symbolic stoning of Judas. If the Jews were believed to have harboured descendants of Judas—and both the name Judas and the term Jew derive from 'Judaean', one who comes from Judaea—perhaps the Jewish people may have been more sympathetic to Jesus. Some scholars believe that Judas himself was just a cipher for the hated Jew.

In their own literature, Jews were occasionally able to make satiric reference to Jesus, himself often a symbol of the plague of Christianity. The most notable Jewish interpretation of Judas is that in the *Toledot Yeshu*. This is an eighth century gospel satire—an interesting approach and one that may resonate with Gnosticism as April de Conick has suggested that the *Gospel of Judas* maybe parodic in its intent.[3] In the *Toledot*, Jesus illegitimately gained access to the divine name, which endowed him with magical powers. The rabbis selected Judah Iskarioto (*sic*) and took him to the temple sanctuary so that he could acquire the same powers for himself. Yeshu demonstrated his magic by lifting up his arms and flying off like an eagle. Judas followed and the two fought, as Judas attempted to force Jesus back down to the ground.

The two were evenly matched, but Judas 'defiled' Jesus (presumably, he performd some action that makes Jesus ritually unclean) and the two of them lost their mastery of the divine name, fell to the earth and died. In other versions, Judas simply outdid Jesus in the magical contest and caused Jesus to lose his knowledge of the divine name. Jesus then had to return to the Jerusalem temple to retrieve it, but on his second visit was captured by the temple authorities.

Judas is not mentioned in the Qur'an, but he is given an unusual role in later Muslim tradition. His part in the story is not necessarily positive, but it adds an intriguing twist to the tale. Sometimes Judas is seen as an heroic figure, deceiving the Jews in an attempt to save Jesus. In the Qur'an Jesus does not die on the cross, a Gnostic theme that lived on in Islamic tradition. Medieval development of this tradition involved a clever variant. In the *Gospel of Barnabas* (a medieval Muslim gospel which seeks to justify Muhammad as the final prophet and the fulfilment of the monotheistic traditions of Abraham, Moses and Jesus that precede him), and also in the writings of a fourteenth-century philosopher named Mba-al-Dimarki, Judas is crucified in the place of Jesus. In *Barnabus*, Jesus is in a room with Judas. As the Sanhedrin or Jewish guards approach, Jesus is spirited away by angels in a deus ex machine and Judas is transformed into the image of Jesus. Judas is thus mistaken for Jesus, taken away and crucified. In the *Gospel of Barnabas*, this is not a heroic sacrifice on the part of Judas, but it is conceivable that the original intention of this Muslim tale of Judas was actually to place Judas in the role of heroically sacrificing himself.

Finally, Irenaeus' account of the *Gospel of Judas* really does present an heroic Judas, a figure who was the result of inverse exegesis by the particular Gnostics (in the accounts of the later heresiologists identified as Cainites) who, at least in the view of the church fathers, eager to make every biblical villain ionto a hero.

However, Judas is only an inverse hero, a hero only by the perverse values of the Gnostics. He was given 'exact knowledge' and knew the truth better than any of the twelve apostles, and through this accomplished the betrayal. Whether Jesus actually wished to be betrayed is not clear in Irenaeus' account—perhaps Judas was the hero, but Jesus the villain?

But it is another version of Judas, in the same work of Irenaeus, but attributed to Valentinians, that Judas is finally and truly redeemed. This is terribly obscure in Irenaeus' account, particularly in the translation in the volumes of the *Ante-Nicene Fathers*, a late Victorian compilation that is still the most easily available text of Irenaeus in English. These Valentinians related a myth in which the twelve apostles are identified with a group of twelve aeons in the pleroma—celestial entities within the divine realm. Judas thus falls from grace in a typological interpretation of the role of Sophia, the aeon who fell from grace and suffered, but eventually was redeemed and returned to the pleroma, setting the pattern of destiny for Gnostics who could also return to the pleroma even though trapped in the material world. Irenaeus objects that Judas wasn't the twelfth disciple but was the thirteenth, and that Judas was not redeemed by died by suicide . But the crux of the story is his redemption. Here we have a genuinely Gnostic account in which Judas falls but is redeemed and therefore has a heroic role. Or perhaps in this Valentinian interpretation he should not be called a hero but the archetypal Gnostic.

Notes

1 Translated by Dr. Tony Chartrand-Burke who teaches Biblical Studies at the Atkinson School of Arts and Letters. http://www.tonychartrand-burke.com/apocryphicity/2008/07/23/the-history-of-the-thirty-pieces-of-silver-given-to-judas/

2 The *Gospel of Philip* plays with a similar idea in section 80, in which Joseph the Carpenter planted the tree and made the cross on which his seed, Jesus, was crucified. I write more on this in *The Gospel of Philip Annotated & Explained*.

3 See April Dr Conick's *The Thirteenth Apostle*, p. 140-147.

A. M. Ashford-Brown

Three Poems

Whose is this assembly of tongues?

Since I cannot remember a time that I haven't been
nor know of any point from which I began
nor am aware of an entity that lives
longer than a thought's span
that I can call 'me'
I wonder

whose is this assembly of tongues
clustered around my pen point,
as I look out into the night,
clamouring for words?

Anima

A volcano spits sparks amid the stars on the edge of night
a dog runs insane in the shadows desire casts about
a snake lies watching a woman at a well eyes dropped
into the water where silver fishes flash in moonlight
and from which she pulls a pail brimming with silvery
luminescence
which overflows and flies away as words she turns
the two halves of the moon in her eyes
to face the flaming sky and smiles
It's for that smile I sweep the sky with nets
for words and birds and stars and sparks to take to her

as little humming odes to tempt her ear
as the shells of the sea

that tell the tales of her legendary heart

The crowned on its steps
the drowned in its depths.

Geese with their home-going

Sad and uncertain
at the sudden onset of autumn
I wander in the evening
I recall my past life—
how have I fared? I shudder.
The seasons turn and the hours pass
yet I do not heed them—
where will they have gone
when the end will be upon me—
the end which will be sudden coming?

The sky in the west is an icy blue streaked with crimson
and geese with their home-going and their mournful cries
haunt me with a desperate longing —
I don't know what it is.

And now I sit by a lantern in a darkened room
rain hitting intermittently the tin roof—
tonight I'm safe - but how many more nights
and where will I be?

A bell strikes the hour and I'm afraid—
I've not yet begun what I came here to do.

Will Parker

Magic and Gnosticism:
An Historical Perspective

Gnosticism might be regarded as a quintessentially *post-modern* impulse, a philosophical response to an existential problem which seems in many ways rather more characteristic of the modern world than the era of cultural antiquity from which it initially emerged. Indeed, 'modern gnosticism' is now acknowledged as a phenomenon in its own right, whose relationship with its classical namesake are rather too complex to be characterised in terms of continuity, revival or reinvention. The intimations of modern Gnosticism are first apparent in the cosmic dilemmas of Goethe's Faust or Milton's Satan. The rumble had become a roar by the start of the nineteenth century, with the psychic battle-cries of William Blake cutting across the din of the industrial revolution. The same sense of post-industrial alienation was articulated (though in very different ways) by Karl Marx and Friedrich Nietzsche, with the liberating possibilities of this existential dislocation later being explored by Søren Kierkegaard and Jean-Paul Sartre. This was the background of the prevailing mood of intellectual 'creative-destruction' that we find advocated by more recent cultural theorists such Jean Baudrillard and Jacques Derrida. From here it is but a small leap into the techno-gnosticism of *The Matrix* or the revolutionary theology of *His Dark Materials*.

So how is it, one might well ask, that a system of thought that seems so enmeshed with the thought-world of classical antiquity seems to anticipate so clearly the 'divine discontent' of modern man? One approach to this problem would be to recognise that classical Gnosticism was initially defined within a particular cultural-historic situation, the key elements of which might be said to have be re-constellating themselves in our own post-industrial, post-colonial era. Whatever its ultimate origins, our earliest knowledge of Gnosticism comes via the hostile gaze of the Church Fathers, who were eager to root out what they saw as the recalcitrant oriental heresy *par excellence*, an embarrassment and an irritant to the universalist aspirations of the rising Roman church. Interestingly enough, the modern Gnosticism of our own times, from Blake onwards, might be seen as the fly in the ointment of another kind of universalist orthodoxy—that of scientific materialism, combined with the western values of democracy and liberal economics. Just as the Church Fathers saw in Gnosticism a veritable witch's cauldron of superstition and cultural deviation, the Gnostic strains of post-modern thought offer scant comfort to the rationalist certainties of our own times. What is challenged on this radical fringe is far more than the socio-political or economic aspects of the liberal capitalist-democracy. What lies at stake are the very underpinnings of what we might call the 'consensus reality' of the post-enlightenment era.

In both cases, then, the Gnostic response has emerged (or been defined) in contradistinction to the prevailing psycho-spiritual dogma, be this the credo of the Roman Church or the scientific materialism of the modern West. In both cases, the dominant brand of occidental universalism has tended to walk hand in hand with the temporal hegemonies of capital and empire, bring with it the promise of security and progress of a material kind. But it is precisely when this *sui disant* progressive universalism

Flower by Scott D. Finch

has started to appear rather like the Blakean 'Nobodaddy' tyrant, something not unlike Gnosticism starts to exert its appeal to the children of the Enlightenment.

The aim of this paper is not take sides in this generational war (so to speak), but rather to understand its deeper historical context—and exactly what is portended by the re-emergence of the Gnostic vision in the modern world. To understand this, we must consider once again that aspect of the human mind that has perhaps always been the fundamental Other in relation to western rationalism. I refer to what we might call 'the magical reality'. Both forms of occidental universalism—whether that of Church fathers of classical antiquity, or that of modern scientific materialism—have a complex relationship with this magical reality (as we shall see), but the effect if not the goal of each has ultimately been excision or neutralisation of this 'irrational' or 'participative' dimension of the human psyche. This goal, when understood in its psycho-historical context, is no more and no less than the profoundly human desire for a kind of ontological stability. The goal of the Gnostic impulse, unconscious or otherwise, might be thought of as a *superhuman* impulse— that is, the desire for a re-integration of the magical reality as a tool of liberation, a means of dissolving this very same ontological stability which some would now argue is now more a prison than a haven for the evolving western mind.   What this re-enchantment of reality ultimately amounts to is a project of *divine self-actualisation*—a sublime if profoundly perilous enterprise. We need to understand not only the magical reality in an anthropological sense but also the *reality of magic* in an ontological sense if we are to understand what was (and is) actually at stake in this radical tension within the western mind.

The crux of the problem comes down to the existence (or otherwise) of *an objective world* which has been fully *revealed*, rather than historically evolved.   So fundamental is the notion of the objective world that we rarely even notice it, let alone question its veracity.

Yet on closer examination this fundamental assumption proves far from conclusive. Here, we will need to take a side-on look at what historical circumstances might have led to the formation of this rationalist consensus-reality, and the nature of the older belief system that it has partially replaced. Only by taking a broader historical view of the modern and pre-modern thought-worlds can we begin to make sense of the significance the Gnostic impulse in our own times.

Anthropologists have written extensively on the subject of magical belief, but few have troubled themselves with the problematic question of the reality or otherwise of magical events. What might be described as the standard positivist response to this problem was expressed unambiguously by Sir James Frazer, author of *The Golden Bough*, a towering figure in early-twentieth century anthropology:

> In short, magic is a spurious system of natural law, as well as a fallacious guide of conduct; it is a false science as well as an abortive art.[1]

So Frazer, and many others after him, regarded magic as a *nothing more* than an expression of falsehood and ignorance, characteristic of the 'savage' mind. In this respect, Frazer was a man of his time. The early twentieth century was the age when confidence in scientific progress (and—related to this—the notion of Western Civilisation itself) was at its zenith. The very idea of the reality of magic was an affront to 'the immutable laws of nature' themselves. This positivist spirit is encapsulated by the attitude of the physicist Hermann von Helmholtz, who once boasted that he was prepared to *utterly reject the evidence of his peers* at the Academy, if their consensus produced a conclusion in favour of the existence of telepathy.[2] Such was the world in which Frazer (whose only contact with non-Western cultures had been through the ethnological documents read in his library) came to shape his conclusions regarding the ontological status of paranormal events.

The mid-twentieth century has brought about significant changes in our understanding of the physical world, both in its sub-atomic constitution on one hand and in terms of the relative nature of time, space and energy on the other. Significantly, too, the nature of *consciousness* itself has emerged as a fundamental problem—one which is arguably insoluble within the conceptual framework of scientific materialism. In the light of these new perspectives, the universe of Newton and Galileo now appears rather less solid and unassailable than it would have done to the leading thinkers of Frazer's generation.

Be this as it may, social anthropologists of today have for the most part retained the default assumption that *all* magical belief must by definition be a fiction. Religious systems continue to be regarded as primarily sociological expressions, perpetuated to consolidate existing power-structures and to enforce communal norms. Magical beliefs are explored only in terms of their interest-value as systems of coercion and behavioural control. Such an approach to the phenomenology of magico-religious expression is useful enough, but only as far as it goes. There can be little doubt that religion *is* an effective form of social control, just it can hardly be denied that where there is magical belief we will often also find ignorance and fraud. However, there is an important body of theoretical and empirical data that needs to be confronted before we can wholly accept this blithe equation between magic and charlatanry, religion and social control.

First, we must appreciate the *universality* of magico-religious belief. For almost the entirety of human history, in nearly every part of the pre-industrial world, the existence of what we would regard as paranormal phenomena has had the status not merely of a theoretical possibility, but as a commonly encountered aspect of everyday experience. By categorically denying the possibility or actuality of this order of reality, the post-industrial West is in a strangely isolated position. If we are to give any credence

whatsoever to the powers of observation among pre-modern humanity, then we need to consider the possibility that this anomaly might be explicable as a difference in perspective (rather than simply a matter of delusion or ignorance) which plays a part in this radical ontological discrepency between the West and the rest of the world.

Also worth noting at this stage are the specific similarities in the reports of magical events across cultures widely separated by time and space. The same array of paranormal phenomena described in the literature of parapsychological research—telekinesis, ecstatic levitation, visual and auditory manifestations—appear with remarkable consistency in the accounts of shamanistic magic from the Arctic to the jungles of sub-Saharan Africa. Stones and other small objects (known to parapsychologists as *apports*) are reported as dropping out of thin air in the sacred places of Aboriginal Australia, just as they do in the poltergeist-haunted homes of Europe or North America. Mysterious lights are sometimes seen flashing across the tree-tops of the African bush, where they are traditionally associated with the activity of sorcerers. The same phenomenon seen in the West might be described as a 'UFO' by anyone inclined towards beliefs of this kind. The terminology and interpretation of these phenomena might vary widely from culture to culture, but the experiences themselves would appear to be remarkably similar.

And nor is it just the hysterical or ignorant who bear witness to this body of anomalous events. Anthropologists, missionaries and other educated Western observers venturing into pre-modern cultural contexts have often reported occurrences that are accepted as perfectly natural by native witnesses, but remain quite inexplicable in terms of conventional science.[3] One such document describes an African practice of drawing a fever out of a human sufferer, by means of a plant or animal proxy:

[The Patient] sweats profusely, then quietly

falls asleep. Meanwhile the animal trembles, shudders and sinks to the ground after a fit of convulsions followed by a sudden stiffening that causes it to topple completely. Usually it is a kid, but sometimes a favourite dog of the patient is used…We saw another sorcerer operate in a similar way. One of our catechism instructors was struck by an algid fever and was gravely ill. Quinine was of no use. The witch-doctor had him carried to an 'Mpala' tree, one that had particularly large leaves, and then he went through his ritual, first over the sick man and then near the tree. The leaves soon started to move and turn black and fall to the ground. The patient sweated a great deal and, the next day, was completely cured.[4]

Interestingly enough, this process of magical transference appears to be a near-universal feature of folk-medicinal traditions throughout the human world.[5] Frazer describes how the natives of Timor, while on long journeys, 'transfer' their fatigue into a leafy branch, which is then thrown away, while the traveller continues his journey with renewed vitality. In parts of the Arab world, headaches are believed to have been transferred to sheep or goats, in a practice similar to that of the African witch-doctors referenced above. Not merely physical symptoms such as fever and fatigue could be transferred in this way; so too could mental illness or even 'bad luck' (widely regarded as a tangible quantity). In Malaysia, a bird flying into the house would be regarded as a bringer of ill-fortune, unless caught, doused with oil, and ritually released, in which case it became a powerful mechanism of removing bad luck from the household. An almost identical practice was known among the women of Ancient Greece, who would anoint and release swallows they caught in their houses, with a similar apotropaic intention. Similar practices involving the transference of illness or misfortune to animals, plants or other inanimate objects have been recorded in the more recent folk-traditions of Europe. A particularly widespread technique involved a lock of hair from patient which was nailed to a beech or an elm, as means of transferring the sickness in a method that is strikingly similar to that of the African witchdoctor described above. Once again, we are reminded that many of these beliefs are all-but universal in the pre-modern world—not just in their general scope, but also frequently in specific matters of detail.

Frazer suggests that folk-medicine is based on a belief in the power of *contagion*, and of the efficacy of homeopathic sympathy (the resemblance of the cause to the effect).[6] However, magical belief cannot be reduced to these principles. To do so would be to ignore the overriding importance of the unseen world of spirits and other magical agencies which permeate these animistic realities. It is this dimension—so acutely apprehended by pre-modern man—that we need to understand in order to penetrate the experience of magical belief.

In many if not most pre-modern societies, a primary channel of contact with the spirit-world was through the agency of a para-epileptic shaman figure, whose seizures are regarded as daemonic possessions, often ritually induced in dramatic communal ceremonies. Such ceremonies, sometimes described by anthropologists as 'seances', lie at the very heart of tribal life. They are typically enacted at religious festivals or other significant moments in the sacred year, or else at critical moments of danger or transition. One such ceremony, which was enacted by a coastal Inuit community during the onslaught of a fierce Arctic gale, was described in detail by the Danish explorer K. Rasmussen:

The Shaman was Horqarnaq, a young man, who took some time to enter into a trance. He explained to Rasmussen that he had several helper-spirits at his disposal: the spirit of his late father; the latter's helper-spirit, an imaginary human figure made out of snow; and a red stone that he had found one day when out hunting. He is dubious about his skills, and is encouraged gently by the village women ... He enters slowly into an almost frenzied trance and the audience increases, trying to stimulate his frenzy ... Finally he no longer recognises the people around him and asks who they are. Then one of the helper spirits enters his body; he no longer has control over his actions; he jumps and dances around, and invokes his father's spirit, an evil spirit. His recently widowed mother is also present, and she tries to calm her son, but others encourage him to greater frenzy. He then names several other spirits of dead people, whom he sees in the hut, among the living. The old women try to guess who it may be, becoming more and more excited as they attempt to solve the mystery. Then one old woman comes forward and calls out the names of the people whom her sisters had not dared to mention: a couple from Nagiutoq who had died quite recently. The shaman cries out that it is they. They have been turned into bad spirits and are the cause of the tempest. The seance goes on for another hour, amid howls and cries and the noise of the storm outside ... Then a fearful thing happens. Horqarnaq leaps at old Kigiuna and seizes hold of him; he shakes him brutally and pushes him into the centre of the hut. They struggle and grunt and eventually he, also, is in a trance and follows the shaman docilely until they fall to the floor where they roll around, possessed. The old man seems to be dead and is dragged over the floor like a sack of old rags ... The tempest has been killed symbolically. The shaman bites the old man and shakes him like a dog would a rat ... The people are silent while Horqarnaq continues his dance ... Then he slowly becomes calmer, kneels down by the body and begins to massage life into it. The old man revives and eventually gets to his feet. But he has only just managed to do this, when the whole scene is repeated, and he is again seized by the throat. This happens three times: three times he is 'killed' in order to show that man is superior to the tempest. Finally, it is the young Shaman

that faints, and the old man rises up and describes the images that are racing before his eyes—naked men and women flying in the air, causing the tempest to swirl before them ... they are afraid and they are fleeing ... Among them is one whom the wind has filled with holes; the wind blows through these, causing the whistling noise ... he is the strongest and will be mastered by the old man's helper-spirit ... Then the young shaman recovers and they both begin to chant and sing plaintively, addressing the Mother of marine animals and begging her to send away the evil spirits, to bite them to death ... So, the two shamans struggle until the tempest is finished, and the people return, reassured, to their huts, prepared to sleep. [7]

Such a scene would doubtlessly shock the modern western observer with its unsettling displays of violence, along with the hysterical participation of the onlookers and the sheer outlandishness of its visionary content. But in all these respects it is not untypical of the shamanic seance as attested throughout the pre-modern world. This widespread ritual form raises a number of interesting questions, some of which will be considered further on in this study, but here what interests us most is the sociological dimension involved. A drama is acted out involving *the loss and regaining of control*, having its corollary in the external communal crisis (in this case, the threatening presence of the Arctic gale). The focus is on the shaman as the point of connection with the unseen spirit world. But in a sense the entire community, both the living and the dead, is drawing together at this moment of crisis. Indeed, it is in this arousal of the communal group-mind and the consequent *dissolution of the barriers between the self and external world*, that we find the factor that comes closest to explaining the magical reality, while at the same time accounting for its relative absence from the modern Western experience.

The spectacle of this dramatised loss of control was a necessarily alarming experience, but nowhere would this be more so than in the secular West. Our cultural outlook might associate such a deranged psychic state with extreme intoxication, or (worse still) with delusional mental illness. Put simply, our civilisation defines itself by behavioural norms for which the shamanic frenzy is the absolute negation. Most other human cultures allow certain occasions wherein a generalised delirium is tolerated if not actively abetted. This is not the case in secular Western society. As a result, 'magical thinking' is confined entirely within the subject: emerging only in the private arena of the dreaming mind, or in the lonely delusions of schizoid mental-illness.

It is probably for this very reason that we have such difficulty appreciating the communal or even collective nature of magico-religious experience in traditional societies. But it is precisely within this field of collective experience—psychic activity that can no longer be described as purely internal—that we find the key to the magical reality. The following account of a magical assault on the Fan, a tribal community in the African bush, illustrates the peculiar ontological status of this category of events:

> The sorcerer went to look at these two people in a dream and saw it was the woman that should die. He called upon the other spirits of his clan to come to his aid and all these spirits left, prepared for war; they left their village and arrived at Akoghengol in the middle of the night. And all of the Fans knew that the spirits were there. The latter seized hold of the woman who then woke up and said to her husband: 'I've just seen the spirits (*beyem*) who have thrown their hunting net over my body'. The husband gave alarm and the whole village awoke. During the night, owls were heard hooting all the way along the road that the spirits had come by. Then the villagers became angry; their spirits also left, prepared for war, and chased away the spirits from the other clan, several of which were wounded by spears thrown during

the night by Fan spears. Two of the other group died. A third one, wounded during the fight, asked a Fan, several days later, 'Is the woman we seized dead?' 'No, but she is very sick,' was the reply. 'She will certainly die,' said the other, 'and because of her, we will also die.' The next day, both the woman and the wounded men were dead.[8]

The background to this conflict lay in the suspected activity of a sorcerer outside the Fan community, who was evidently looking for a victim on to which to 'transfer' the sickness of one of his clients. But what is so extraordinary about this account is that a large proportion of the subsequent action apparently takes place in a dimension that cannot be adequately defined exclusively in purely physical or psychological terms. It is best understood (from our point of view) as a kind of 'shared dreamspace' accessible to the entire bush community, Fan and non-Fan alike. But even this definition is not entirely adequate. Given the evident psycho-somatic effect of these telepathic experiences, we need to accept that this 'shared dreamspace' also interpenetrates the *material* world, to the extent that injuries sustained during these nightly magical conflicts can even result in the physical death of the participants involved. For the Fan, and other pre-modern peoples, it was enough to simply accept that one's spirit would sometimes wander freely at night—where it would interact with other corporeal and non-corporeal entities. This was the basis of the magical reality.

The Italian anthropologist Ernesto de Martino made a study of this problem in a controversial monograph, from which many of the accounts quoted above have been drawn.[9] De Martino's conclusion from this data was that 'the self' as we know it is a largely cultural construct, particular to the historical circumstances of the post-industrial West. As a fixed concept it is less applicable to pre-modern contexts, where its existence is altogether more precarious. For an example of the primitive instability of the ego-self De Martino refers to a distinctive mental condition known as *koinonia* (communion)[10], described by a number of anthropologists in the context of Asiatic Siberia and the Melanesian islands (variants of which also are also evident in medieval Europe, as we shall see below).

Known as *latah* among the Malay, *olon* by the Tungus or *imu* by the Ainus, this altered state of consciousness (which is most often experienced after shock or profound emotional upheaval) results in a comprehensive breakdown of psychic cohesion. The subject loses all control over himself and his actions. More significantly perhaps, *all sense of separation between himself and the outside world* necessarily breaks down. If his attention is caught by branches moving in the wind, he will compulsively imitate this movement; if someone else around him starts running on the spot, he will do the same. De Martino remarks of this curious psychic state:

It is as if there is some element present that surrenders itself completely to an outside force … as if this insecure, unstable presence is unable to withstand the shock of some emotive force … his fragile 'control' reaches an 'impasse' that it is incapable of surmounting, so it abandons all effort. When this barrier is down, there is no longer any distinction between his control and the action that he sees: instead of hearing or seeing the rustling of leaves in the wind, he *becomes* the tree that has the rustling leaves … in this psychic situation, the peculiar 'presence' within the individual acts as an echo of the world[11]

De Martino sees the relative stability of the self or 'presence' in Western man as the outcome of a particular process of historical evolution, rather than an *a priori* condition of humanity as a whole. The state of koinonia described above testifies to a cultural situation in which this presence is noticeably less secure. Magic, according to de Martino, is wholly symptomatic of this unstable psychic situation:

When the presence resists [the onset of koinonia] because it wants to be free to function, a typical and easily-recognisable type of anguish is produced. The presence may then become aware of the need to redeem itself, and it does this by creating certain cultural forms [i.e. magical rituals]. If the presence fades, without any effort or reaction taking place, then the magic world has not yet appeared. If the presence is redeemed and consolidated and is no longer aware of its fragile nature, then the magic world has already disappeared. It is between these two states that the magic world makes its appearance—in the struggle and opposition that arise between them— here, the magic world becomes manifest as movement and development: it displays its many cultural forms and is born into the history of mankind.[12]

Placing magic in the context of this existential drama helps us apprehend the experience in subjective terms. But, as we have seen, to its original practitioners magic was more than just a psychological exercise for the maintaining of inner poise. The psychodrama of crisis and redemption, enacted by the shaman, is simultaneously also an operation with *objective* goals: frequently being triggered in response to a threat to the community such as the Arctic gale menacing the Inuit as described above. The paranormal phenomena surrounding shamanic activity might be seen as a projection or extension of the ontological turmoil experienced by the threatened presence, a conflict which is then manifest in the 'shared dreamspace' of the community involved. The storm and the shamanic turmoil were one and the same—no distinction is made between these two orders of reality. The shaman acts out the drama of his psychic dissociation for the duration of the storm; and concludes his restitution to ego-consciousness as the storm abates. In doing so he is able to redeem his community: demonstrating human mastery over a threat that is simultaneously psychic and external. As

De Martino explains:

> Corresponding to the magical risk of *losing the soul*, there exists the danger of *losing the world*. Together with the experience of the soul that leaves its abode and is attacked, compromised, violated, etc., we have the experience of objects that go beyond their tangible horizons, escape from their limits and fall into chaos... When considered in this light, magic becomes a restorative power that brings back threatened horizons, and returns the world to mankind.[13]

The ultimate aim of the magical endeavour, according to De Martino, is the attainment of 'a presence that is guaranteed in its relationships to a balanced, ordered world'. The latter, it might be said, is the psychological and ontological state now securely inhabited by Western man. Through the development of certain intellectual tools, *we have objectified reality* by successfully disengaging the subject. The end result is a secure and predictable world which no longer presents a threat to our existential integrity. In the context of European history, the role of organised religion—regarded by some as the intermediary stage of between the magical and the scientific world view—might be seen as a significant factor in the complex process of psychic individuation which has led to the development of modern 'objectified' consciousness. About this process, we will have more to say below. But first we must return to the issue of Gnosticism, and its relationship to the ontological journey of the western mind.

Gnosticism, as we have seen, was initially defined by its enemies. We first hear the term in the description of a heretical movement by the Church fathers, during the early centuries of the Christian era (its origins before this time are beyond the scope of this paper). It was during this era that the Church was attempting to impose a greater uniformity of custom and belief, and acquire the characteristics of a Universal Church rather than disparate network of oriental cults. The more contemplative elements in Eastern Mediterranean Christianity, which often combined the theology of the Gospel of John with other less familiar elements such as the dualistic doctrines of the Persian Manicheans and the neo-Platonic echoes of the ancient pagan world, were no longer as acceptable to this new Orthodoxy, which prized faith and conformity above mystical enquiry and personal revelation. Matters came to a head in 367 when a Christian mob burned down the ancient library of Alexandria, which contained a sizable body of Gnostic manuscripts. The same year saw the 'Barbarian Conspiracy', in which the western empire was subject to a co-ordinated series of attacks from a disparate alliance of Germanic and other barbarian groups on its north and western fringes. It is in this year that the medieval era can be said to have begun.

As might be imagined, the conflagration at Alexandria and the advent of the Barbarian assault on the Western empire signalled the descent into an altogether rougher and less philosophical age. But even before this time, the classical civilisation that produced urbane rationalists such as Cicero and Seneca had long since disappeared. The Emperor Constantine made Christianity the official religion of the Empire 312 years after the birth of the Saviour, leading to a cultural change which was merely confirmed by the events of 367. Thereafter, blind faith and communal piety were the keynotes of the prevailing psycho-spiritual climate, rather than reason or esoteric inquiry. Within such a world there was less room for the educated, idiosyncratic mysticism of second century Gnostics such as Basilides or Valentinus of Alexandria.

So where did the psyche of the medieval Christian abide on the spectrum represented by the compulsive instinctuality of the primitive koinoniac on one hand, and the empirical ego-consciousness of the post-industrial Westerner on the other? In many respects, the medieval era has rightly been regarded as a step backwards into the kind of benighted superstition that we might associate with the magical reality in all its least appealing extremes. With the collapse of the apparatus of empire, Europe quickly descended into a primitive society of illiterate, near-subsistence farmers—heavily exploited by a warlike feudal elite. In many respects, particularly within the rustic peasant communities, we might expect to encounter a mental world closer to that of the African Fan or the Arctic Inuit than the modern-day post-industrial consciousness. Despite lacking a substantial documentary record of the thoughts and opinions of the illiterate majority in medieval Europe, we can now be sure that a superstitious belief in the spirit-world constituted an important dimension of the popular world-view. So much is clear from the folk-medicine recorded in such works as the Old English *Lacununga*[14] or the Wolfstan manuscript[15]: handbooks written in the local vernacular, often combining quasi-Christian invocatory formulae with traditional herbal knowledge; pseudo-astrology with magical charms of apparent pagan derivation.

Beyond this, even into the late medieval and early modern period, we hear of outbreaks of mass-hysteria in Continental Europe such as that of the *flagellantes* around the middle of the fourteenth century, which hint at the borderline group-mind experiences characteristic of magical belief as described above. The seventeenth-century rumours of satanic nocturnal sabbaths, although prompted and sustained by self-appointed clerical inquisitors, bear an uncanny resemblance to the witch-lore of the Azande as described by twentieth-century anthropologist E. E. Evans-Pritchard.[16] Some of the more outlandish peasant rebellions of the fifteenth century exhibit the characteristics of a cult-movement, reminiscent of the magical secret-societies of the African bush. Most significantly, perhaps, the well-documented phenomena of exorcism and demonic possession suggest that the spiritual threat to the 'presence' was still a tangible problem for the medieval subject.

At a popular level, Christianity offered a battery of magical solutions to bolster the security of the presence—not just the abjurations of the caster of demons (of whom Jesus Christ himself was the earliest exemplar); but also the protective talismans of the crucifix and the rosary, as well as the delineation of time and space into the sacred and non-sacred, through which sanctuary could be found for the threatened ego consciousness. The sense of the demon-haunted darkness that lies beyond these fragile islands of security is implicitly evoked in the opening scene of *Hamlet*, as the terrified guards witness the ghost of the dead king fade at the break of dawn:

It faded on the crowing of the cock!
Some say that ever 'gainst that season comes
Wherein our Saviour's birth is celebrated,
The bird of dawning singeth all night long:
And then, they say, no spirit dares stir abroad;
The nights are wholesome; then no planets
 strike,
No fairy takes, nor witch hath power to
 charm,
So hallow'd and so gracious is the time.

So, even during the life of Shakespeare, human experience was still divided into 'hallowed' and 'non-hallowed' time. During the hours of night, the stability of the ego (and with it, the fabric of reality itself) threatens to unravel, with disturbing unconscious elements (spirits, witches, malign astral forces) projected outwards into the surrounding darkness.

Yet, for all its thuggish anti-intellectualism and superstitious mummery, it is to Christianity that we owe the foundation—if not the actualisation—of the consciousness of the modern world. The shattered fragments of antiquity were preserved in the monasteries of the Early Medieval West, and it was out of these remnants that the sacred flame of literacy (a key element in the historical transformation of human consciousness) was kept alive. By the late Middle Ages, men such as Roger Bacon (d.1294), John Duns Scotus (d.1308) and William of Ockham (d. 1347)—just three of a number of highly literate university-educated thinkers emerging in Western Europe at the time—were in the process of reforming the study of logic, language and the philosophy of science, which had hitherto been kept alive merely through the preservation of these fragments of antiquity in Europe and the Muslim world over the last eight hundred years.[17] The scholastic tradition in which these men worked was essentially an outgrowth of the pedagogic disciplines of the monastic curriculum.[18] Medieval intellectual activity remained close to its theological roots throughout the period. For men such as Roger Bacon and John Scottus, reason was the handmaiden of faith; and learning, even the study of philosophers of pagan antiquity, was a legitimate means of illuminating religious understanding. Taking their cue from the writings of Plato and Aristotle, the medieval scholar reflected deeply on what might seem to us rather doctrinaire questions: the age and the dimensions of the created universe; the relation between the 'accidents and essences'; the scope and limitations of human knowledge. But by nurturing and developing these lines of thought, they were situating the human subject as a passive observer within the framework of *an objective, interpretable universe*. It was this achievement that enabled the stabilisation (or disengagement) of the subject, and the consequent growth of scientific knowledge that took place in the post-medieval West.[19] Whether they realised it or not, these scholastic thinkers were laying the foundations of the modern western mind.

The period from the late fourteenth to the end of the sixteenth centuries saw, among other things, the re-discovery of the classical past and the heliocentric Copernican cosmology—the first significant challenge to the intellectual authority of the Roman church. The centuries that followed, the so-called Enlightenment period, saw a succession of thinkers from Descartes to Voltaire arguing for the sovereignty of reason over superstition. Galileo and Newton had added concepts such as gravity, the solar system and the experimental method to the sum of human knowledge. Eighteenth-century

inventions such as the spinning jenny, the power loom and finally the steam engine offered intimations of an industrial future. Reason, it seemed, had triumphed over superstition. Progress, of a rational and beneficial kind, appeared to be the order of the day.

It was some time before these notions of progress and enlightenment had any tangible impact on the inner or outer world of the majority population—most of whom continued to live as subsistence in small-scale rustic communities well into the nineteenth century. However, by the end of the eighteenth century the pieces were in place, and the political and industrial revolution became an unavoidable feature of the contemporary social landscape, drawing increasing numbers into its orbit. The modernisation of agricultural techniques and land-ownership rights drove many off the land and into the factory. Meanwhile, the violent deposition of the *ancien regime* along with the awe-inspiring power of the industrial machine insured that the old symbolic order was not so much dead and buried, as decapitated and incinerated in a factory furnace. The Middle Ages were well and truly at an end.

'God is dead' wrote Nietzsche in 1882 'and we have killed him.' The question raised by Nietzsche in this oft-quoted but frequently misunderstood passage was how to retain any system of values in the absence of a Divine order. Less problematic, however, was the issue of the ontological framework that would replace the discredited Christian cosmology. The nineteenth century was something of a time of wonders in terms of scientific discovery, and what had begun life as a set of investigative methodologies soon acquired the status of a fully-blown belief system. Scientific materialism has become the indisputable religion of our times. In conjunction with the spread of literacy, the universal provision of state education, this very particular view of the nature of existence has engineered a profound alteration in the apparatus of western consciousness and its relationship with the world. As summed up most succinctly by the philosopher Martin Buber, we have moved from an 'I-Thou' relationship with the world into a state of solipsistic alienation— the 'I-It' reality in which no consciousness is recognised beyond the human ego.

As late as the 1970s, it was possible to believe that the stream of technological miracles would continue as it had done since the industrial revolution. The dream of space travel typified this spirit of benign scientism. Humankind would physically launch itself out into the stars. New worlds of endless possibility would be discovered and colonised, allowing us to leave behind the mundane problems of overpopulation and environmental ruin. Spatial distance would be blithely spanned, if not by teleportal devices then at least by superior rocket power. Most promisingly of all, contact would surely be made with technologically advanced civilisations from other planets, offering a short-cut to technological utopia. Early estimations concluded that tens if not hundreds of thousands of such alien civilisations would exist within our own galaxy alone. Surely it was simply a matter of time before the radio signals from our planet would be picked up by some neighbourly aliens and contact would be made? As a corollary to this assumption, scientists have been tuning in to the background electromagnetic radiation of outer space since the 1960s, looking out for any anomalies or signals which might indicate the activity of intelligent life beyond the solar system.

Forty years on, however, no such signal has been traced. This deafening radio silence seems to underline the increasing realisation of the sheer scale and emptiness of space, and our apparent isolation within it. Even with the most powerful equipment available to our civilisation, it would take 64,000 years to reach our nearest solar system. We have seen how already how aberrant or primitive patterns of consciousness seem to imitate, alter or even *determine* the nature of the surrounding reality. We might note that the cosmology of scientific materialism has come to represent the planet in precisely the same state of lonely isolation as the ego finds itself within the sterile vacuum of the I-It reality.

As we have already implied, with the advance of empirical science comes the solidification, the objectification, the *ossification* of the material universe. This has perhaps been a necessary phase in the evolution of the western mind. No-one can witness the ravages of schizophrenia, or consider the hysterical violence of the witch-hunting mob, without being grateful for the advent of Enlightenment. No can one neglect the material benefits, too numerous to mention, which have been accrued through the dedicated application of scientific investigation.

And yet we are left with a lingering sense of loss. *'Is this all there is?'* seems to be the refrain of the twenty-first-century West—well-fed, innoculated and spiritually bereft. The cosmic and moral metaphors of scientific materialism— Black Holes; the Big Bang and the Big Crunch; the Blind Watchmaker and the Selfish Gene— reinforce this state of post-modern alienation. If this is indeed 'all there is', it seems we have little more to look forward to than the inevitable Malthusian crunch between the profligate, aging populations of the developed world and the hungry, resource-starved majority in the poorer regions of this overcrowded planet. The prospects for what we used to refer to as Western Civilisation would appear increasingly bleak.

However, while history testifies to the rise and fall of civilisations, it also contains another significant lesson, what Thomas Kuhn referred to as *the paradigm shift* in human thought and systems of social organisation. Whether or not we endorse Kuhn's theory as originally set out in *The Structure of Scientific Revolutions*, it is hard to seriously sustain the view that further radical revisions to our understanding of ourselves and the reality we inhabit are impossible or even particularly unlikely. In other words, the notion that 'this is all there is' is not only morbidly inimical to human creativity and imagination— it is also profoundly unrealistic. *There will be more*—and it is merely a matter of time before we find where and how to look for it.

The limiting aspects of scientific-materialist

paradigm were already being apprehended by the likes of John Keats, who wrote the following oft-quoted lines in 1820:

Do not all charms fly
At the touch of cold philosophy?
Philosophy will clip an Angel's wings,
Conquer all mysteries by rule and line,
Empty the haunted air, and gnomed mine—
Unweave a rainbow, as it erewhile made
The tender-person'd Lamia melt into a shade.

This quote, all too often taken out of context, does not advocate the abandonment of the scientific method, but warns of the perils of its decouplement from the wide spectrum of human sensibility. The eponymous 'Lamia' of this poem represents the opposite danger—complete abandonment to the irrational world of emotional instinctuality. Keats seems to recognise the need to move beyond this magical reality, but recognises the price that will be paid in doing so.

In the previous generation William Blake had offered a blunter assessment. He had reviled the *bien pensants* of the Enlightenment ('Mock on, mock on, Voltaire Rousseau!') as enthusiastically as he disdained against the black-frocked minions of organised religion. He referred to atheism as 'Satan's Doctrine', singling out Newton, Bacon and Locke as its unholy triumvirate. His description of Newton's worldview as 'the single vision' (as opposed to the 'four-fold vision' of the spiritual man) presents an uncomfortable reminder of the undoubted truth that scientific enquiry has relied on a *narrowing* of the frames of reference, a *shutting-down* of certain paraxial modes of perception.

From the margins of history, science and western civilisation, where the magical reality can still hold sway, strangely persistent accounts continue to emerge which undermine our certainty that we know all that there is to be known about the human mind and its relationship with reality. It has not been possible to offer any convincing, cast iron proof of the paranormal, yet neither can the objective observer categorically dismiss the fact that (in historical terms) the overwhelming majority of humanity believe themselves to have experienced the reality of magic. Many would argue for the preservation of the ego-bound 'I-It' consciousness characteristic of the modern western mind, for which a denial of the magical reality is a key ingredient. To explore such things we need to enter realms of conscious experience that border perilously with the delusions of the schizophrenia, or the helpless abandon of koinoniac. As William Blake once suggested, 'unless the mind catch fire/the God will not be known.'

Gnosticism, past and present, might be seen as an exercise in kindling this flame. *Gnosis* in its initiatory sense meant direct experience of the godhead—an experience that was by necessity brutally overwhelming and fundamentally life-changing. The challenge for the Gnostic today is to re-kindle this fire, but to do so in a way which does not jeopardise the hard-won security of ego-consciousness. The new frontier may well prove to be that of inner space—which may well turn out to be less distinct from outer space than was previously realised. What is needed is not a regression into the dark waters of the shamanic frenzy or the daemonic koinonia, but rather the pioneering of new 'techniques of ecstasy' which are both effective and appropriate for the modern mind. Perilous though it might be to venture forth into these powerful and transformative states of consciousness, this may indeed be what it takes to rediscover the way out of the illusory prison of three-dimensional space, and remake that vital connection with the living reality on which our survival may increasingly depend.

Notes

1 Frazer, Sir James *The Golden Bough—A Study in Magic and Religion*, Abridged Edition, London 1925 p.11

2 De Martino, infra (n. ##) p.120

3 This problem was noted parenthetically by South African anthropologist Philip Mayer ('Witches' in *Witchcraft and Sorcery*, ed. Max Marwick, Harmondsworth: Penguin 1970, p. 49) 'More often than not there is no positive evidence, but even so things happen in the field that shake one's scepticism. Like Evans-Pritchard (1937), I have seen among the *gusii* at night: suggestive lights moving near my camp, lights that died down and flared up exactly as the witchcraft myth alleges.'

4 R. G. Trilles *Les Pygmées de la forêt equatorial*. Paris, 1932, pp.177-178. Quoted in translation by De Martino (infra) p. 29.

5 Frazer ibid pp.543-546

6 Frazer, ibid., p.11 ff.

7 K. Rasmussen 'Intellectual Culture of the Igluick Eskimos' Report of the 5th Thule Expedition 1921-24 VII, no. 1, Copenhagen 1929. Quoted in translation in de Martino, pp. 108-109

8 This account was relayed by Mba Eyana, a member of the Fan community, and told to the missionary Charles Cadier, who later relayed it to the anthropologist Raoul Allier (*Le civilseé et nous*, Paris 1927, pp. 291 ff). It is quoted, in translation in de Martino (infra, n.36) p.127

9 Ernesto de Martino *Primitive Magic—The Psychic Powers of the Shamans and Sorcerers* (Dorset: Prism Press, 1998).

10 This might be compared to the more general phenomenon of 'disassociation'.

11 De Martino (1998) p.68

12 De Martino (1998) p.70

13 De Martino (1998) p.111

14 Edited and translated by Godfrid Storms in *Anglo-Saxon Magic* (The Hague: Nijhoff, 1948)

15 This text is discussed by Richard Kieckhefer in *Magic in the Middle Ages* (Cambridge: CUP, 2000) pp. 3-5

16 *Witchcraft, Oracles and Magic among the Azande* (Oxford: Clarendon Press, 1937)

17 For a comprehensive review of the medieval intellectual tradition from classical antiquity to the renaissance see David Luscombe *Medieval Thought* OUP: Oxford, New York, 1997)

18 The programme which became known as 'the liberal arts' had been developed by scholars such as Alcuin of York in Carolignian France from the eighth century onwards. This in turn was a continuation of the educational programmes of classical antiquity—using ancient textbooks written by men such as Cassidorus (d. c.580) and Isidore of Seville (d.636). The seven liberal arts consisted of the *trivium* (grammar, dialectic and rhetoric) and the *quadrivium* (arithmetic, geometry, astronomy and music). Alcuin described these as 'the seven columns which hold up the temple of Christian wisdom' (Luscombe, 1997, pp. 29-31).

19 The meeting point of theology and science came with the characteristically Western concept of the 'laws of nature', itself an outgrowth of the idea of rational, law-giving Deity, as Paul Davies explains: 'In Renaissance Europe, the justification for what we might call the scientific approach to inquiry was the belief in a rational God whose created order could be discerned from a careful study of nature. And, Newton notwithstanding, part of this belief came to be that God's laws were immutable. 'The scientific culture that arose in Western Europe,' writes Barrow, 'of which we are the inheritors, was dominated by adherence to the absolute invariance of the laws of Nature, which thereby underwrote the meaningfulness of scientific enterprise and assured its success'...it is interesting to ponder whether science would have flourished in medieval and Renaissance Europe were it not for Western theology.' (*The Mind of God—Science and the Search for the Ultimate Meaning* London: Penguin Books, 1992 p. 77)

Miguel Conner

Sethian Gnosticism:
An Interview with John Turner

John Turner is Professor of Religious Studies and Professor of Classics and History at the University of Nebraska-Lincoln and a world expert in Sethian Gnosticism. Several of his translations of Nag Hammadi texts were included in both the Nag Hammadi Library in English and its successor The Nag Hammadi Scriptures. He is the author of many books and articles on Gnosticism. This interview was conducted by Miguel Conner for Coffee, Cigarettes and Gnosis and is also available in its original audio format at http://thegodabovegod.com.

MC: Could you give us just a brief overview of the origins and theology of Sethian Gnosticism?

JT: I can try. It's a rather complicated sort of thing, and, as you know, often when one deals with these kinds of materials, why, you sometimes get lost in the details. But in some way some of the details are important because Sethianism is probably, I would say, the earliest form of gnosticism for which we have a good deal of documentation. And it seems to be a forerunner of Valentinianism, and there is some relationship between some of the elements of Valentinian mythology and Sethian mythology as well. Some people prefer to call Sethian mythology or Sethian Gnosticism classical Gnosticism, also the approach of Bentley Layton in his book *The Gnostic Scriptures*, which is a very nice collection of material.

MC: The question most people would have is: is the Sethian Gnosticism the fountainhead of Gnosticism, or is it something that went after, let's say, Simon Magus and Saturnalius and Menander. Where exactly does it fall into or do we really know?

JT: We don't really know and that's the problem, of course, actually, with many of those Gnostic theologies that stem from the people that you mentioned. Simon Magus, of course was regarded as the arch heretic, because he was the earliest one whose existence the church fathers were able to establish by identifying him with the figure in Acts Chapter 8, the one who called himself a great power, and so the heresiologists, when they deal with this, in some way model the development of Gnosticism on their own conception of, their model of, the church which was, more or less, hierarchically organized and which they conceived as a kind of sequence of bishops who presided over various provinces and so that's, kind of, the way they look at Gnosticism as well, as a kind of tree, stemming then from the earliest figures they could come up with, such as, beginning of course, obviously, with Simon Magus and then some of the other figures who *do* seem to be early although precise time of origin is undocumented. But one might think of Basilides, Menander, and others that you just mentioned. So the problem with Sethianism of course is that we have no figure that we can identify as the founder of this movement. None of the Sethian Gnostic documents, with the possible exception of a rather late one called *Marsanes*, seem actually to mention a specific Gnostic teacher. In a way wandering around in a kind of vague wonderland of ideas.

MC: Right.

JT: In general the Gnostics, then, do not like to talk about themselves, say, as a social group and, in fact, it's even debated as to whether it's fair to say that they actually had a self-identification. So, for example, then when you hear about Sethians and Valentinians, what you're dealing with are names which the church fathers have chosen to designate them. But nevertheless, we could get at least to what I think to be the rough history of this movement. It seems to me that, it's arguable that Sethianism had its origin, I think, in some kind of Jewish priestly movement. I'm thinking mainly among those priestly groups which became, rather gradually, excluded from leadership in the Temple, especially during the second and third century, second and first centuries BCE and the Temple was taken over of course by the Zadokite priestly establishment.

MC: Right.

JT: And this, of course, you probably discussed with others, things about the Dead Sea Scrolls

MC: Right

JT: And that's, the community, then would be an example of a kind of priestly community, which simply left then the area of Jerusalem, perceiving the Temple to have actually been politicised and polluted. So they then went to the wilderness, in order then that they could worship God in the true heavenly Temple, rather than the— what they regarded as—the corrupted earthly Temple. And, I think, I would tend to see the antecedence of Sethianism then among such groups, since it's clear that the Sethians have a great interest really in the transcendent world. Their view of the transcendent world, essentially, is centred around the notion of kind of supreme trinity which is called often just simply Father, Mother and Child. The Father then is the one that they normally call the Great Invisible Spirit, the Mother is the figure called Barbelo a name that we can't really decipher for sure

MC: Ah that's exactly one of the burning questions I had, because I heard so many different, so many different versions. I thought you might have, you have the one, John.

JT: No, I don't really have the one. There are probably about six rather distinctive attempts to understand this name. Probably the one that people, I guess, mention the most would

be that it's some kind of smoothing out of a phrase something like B-arba-Eloh, that is 'In Four is God'—the idea that Barbelo originally represented the divine Tetragrammaton—God. Because during this period there was a lot of speculation on the divine name—the name of course was important because in these days when God was thought of as so highly transcendent, above the world of ordinary human endeavour, the question then arose then, how could God possibly then relate, from such an exalted level, to humanity?

And therefore there were various attributes of God, which people thought were the means by which God did in some way relate to the earthly environment. The name of God for example, or the temple of God, the so called Shekinah, for those who held onto the earthly Temple, the idea of the glory of God which dwelt in the Temple and so on. It may be that the origin of the Barbelo name goes back to some idea of this sort. But it's clear though that, in Sethianism, that Barbelo was almost an entirely transcendental mother figure and acts then more or less then as the consort of the high deity, the Invisible Spirit. Then to complete the Trinity you then have the figure of the self-generated Child, who is, of course, a very interesting figure because this is the one in which essentially a kind of heterodox Jewish form of speculation becomes then gradually identified with Christ as the Sethian tradition then becomes christianised, that is, essentially enters into some kind of relationship with the Christians. In any case, I try to suggest this may have happened in roughly five or six stages so that you begin then with this group, who—I'm not sure whether they were very aware of a distinctive Jewish identity—but I think that they certainly arose from that kind of general milieu of worship in the heavenly Temple, which of course then accounts for the very heavy occurrence of acts of vision and acts of liturgical praise and so forth which occurs in the various Sethian documents. Of course one could therefore use a convenient designation, since Barbelo seems to be the distinctive name, and it's clear that the earliest reports that we have of their thinking come to us from the hands of Irenaeus, who wrote his work *Against the Heresies* probably somewhere around 175CE, and he refers to these people simply then as Gnostics. 'A multitude of Gnostics' is the term which he uses. But it soon became customary then for those people who used Irenaeus as a source then to try to make Irenaeus' identifications more precise and so we find that, very early on, the term Barbeloite applied to this very first group of Gnostics which Irenaeus discusses. Irenaeus of course begins with a lengthy discussion of the Valentinians, tries to say something about Valentinus and other valentinian teachers, Marcus for instance. But then by the time he gets to the end of the first book of his work *Against the Heresies,* in chapter 29, he then talks about another multitude of Gnostics. And so this is the group then that became later more precisely identified as Barbeloites. What's interesting about these people, their hallmark, seems to have been a communal rite, baptismal immersion—more than likely in ordinary water—that somehow resulted in an experience of transcendental vision, which was thought then to lead to complete enlightenment and total salvation. This ritual was called the Five Seals and many explanation have been provided, but I'm not really positively sure myself why they actually called it the Five Seals because, depending on which of the Sethian treatises you read, you can account for the number five in various ways. But certainly the term 'seal' is significant and does suggest therefore some connection with baptism which early on For example, baptism in Christianity was always considered a sort of sealing…

MC: Ah-hah!

JT: An initiation, that kind of thing. So, in any case, the rite was important because it was thought of as the instrument of salvation that had actually been conferred by the divine mother Barbelo, understood as a kind of universal mother. She was thought of as the First Thought, a kind of projection of the divine mind, of the supreme deity called the Invisible Spirit and so then together with the Invisible Spirit, Barbelo then conceives the third member of the Sethian trinity, who was called the self-generated child, represented actually by the Greek word Autogenes, which simply means 'self-generated' or 'self-begotten' and then, very briefly, the, this child then goes on to establish essentially the heavenly realm which consists of four angelic luminaries and I won't go into the details of that but one of these luminaries then finally, and usually the fourth of these, becomes the resident of the figure of Sophia, whom I'm sure you and your guests have discussed frequently.

MC: Very much so, yes

JT: Who then becomes responsible, ultimately, for the origin of the world by giving rise to the world Creator and the story then continues from that point on. So, in any case that seems to represent a kind of first stage of things, as far as I can see, in this sort of general history of development of Sethianism but before I stop, there's a second very important component which is probably the one that most people who read about gnosticism are familiar with, and this is, of course, the very large role which the interpretation of the initial books of Genesis especially Genesis 2 through 9 play in their story of primordial times. My own sense is that this comes probably from slightly different quarters than this kind of Barbeloite baptismal speculation

MC: Really?

JT: Yes, I think so. Probably, again we can use Irenaeus as a guide because, as I say, towards the end of Book 1 in chapter 29 then he discusses these Gnostics who were later identified by people like Theodoret as Barbeloites and then in chapter 30 he then discusses a mythological system which likewise, he says, is typical of other Gnostics, and then later on people like Theodoret and Pseudo-Tertullian identify these people as Ophites mainly, because they thought that the Ophites had a particular interest in the serpent of Paradise acting as the healer and *ophis* in Greek, where you get the word Ophite, is a word for snake or a serpent. And so, Irenaeus then discusses these views in the succeeding chapter, Chapter 30, but it's quite clear that their sort of metaphysics and theology of the highest transcendental realm is very different than what we see in the Sethians. Sethians have the supreme trinity, whereas these people who became called Ophites actually have a kind of supreme pentad or group of five deities—essentially four male deities and a female deity as well. The female deity of course proving to be Sophia, and in the Ophite system the main actor in salvation is the figure of Sophia, whereas in the Sethian treatises the main actor in salvation is the figure of Barbelo who was distinguished quite clearly from Sophia. Barbelo and Sophia share certain, of course, share in common their *femaleness*, but quite often you see that in the Sethian treatises, that Barbelo is usually called male. She's the male virgin. And in fact in later stages of Sethianism she actually becomes no longer called Barbelo but the aeon of Barbelo and aeon of course is a masculine term. And so it gets you then into some of the background of all of this, the very interesting role then of female deities in Gnostic systems, who usually of course end up representing something about origin of the world of becoming, some element of unpredictability, some element of daring, some element of deficiency, whereas the male on the other hand then tends more to symbolise permanence and stability, predictability and things of this sort. So Barbelo is a very interesting figure because clearly she's a positive figure, but nevertheless she does represent the first stage of the emergence from this supreme invisible spirit—who is generally thought to be male—which then obviously allows everything else to come into being

MC: So would you say for example; the Secret Book of John has both Barbelo and Sophia, are you saying that they were actually maybe two different stories put together? Or is there…

JT: Well it could partly be so. The apocryphon—you 're very right to bring up that document because if you were to read these chapters in book 1 of Irenaeus' work *Against the Heresies*, chapter 29 and 30 in sequence, you would see that it matches up quite well with the two really major sections of the *Apocryphon of John*. One might well wonder then whether the *Apocryphon of John* was produced as a kind of fusion of these two theologies which I mentioned, the trinitarian theology of the sort of Barbeloites, these proto- Sethians, and this kind of midrash on the paradise story on the part of these other Gnostics who became called Ophites, who themselves have a kind of supreme group of five deities rather than the Sethian trinity. And so the kind of material then that you read in what's traditionally called Irenaeus' Ophites then seems to correspond roughly to much of the second half of the *Apocryphon of John,* whereas the Barbeloite material seems to correspond roughly with the first part of the *Apocryphon of John*; the first part treating mainly the transcendental word on down say to it's periphery, at the periphery of the realm of the four lights, where we find Sophia. Sophia then deciding that she wants to somehow emulate the creative power of the highest deity, produces an accident because she doesn't cooperate with her male partner or aspect, which then produces the world creator or Yaldabaoth and then, of course, everything devolves from that point and that then leads directly to the paradise midrash as soon as Yaldabaoth and his fellow rulers decide then to create the first human being.

MC: And it's seems it's probably even more complicated because, as Stevan Davies posited, I don't know if you agree with this but the *Secret Book of John* was than later christianised, so you might have three sticky fingers in there…

JT: Well, that's conceivable, that is I *do* think that the original milieu of these ideas of a kind of supreme trinity, a heavenly world, a heavenly world of lights and this sort of baptismal ritual of the five seals, does in a way seem to be not in its origin specifically Christian, despite the fact of course that Christianity went on to posit its own Trinitarian theology. But it seems to me that it begins roughly in a kind of movement in the fringes of Judaism mainly among a kind of disenfranchised priestly component, who devised this kind of view of the divine world and essentially adopted, or *adapted*, the priestly rites of lustration, which were always traditional to a kind of act of baptism which is mainly designed to produce acts of vision, that is, vision of the transcendent world, vision of the beings that populate it. All of these beings of course emerging ultimately from the high deity, and as they emerge they engage in acts of praise like choirs of angels of the sort, for example, that we read of in much Jewish pseudepigraphical literature as well. That, it certainly does reach a point—and my sense would be that this certainly must happen in the second half of the first century—that this movement definitely then intersects with Christianity, you might say that it becomes christianised. We don't know anything about the process by which this may have happened, but by and large it does seem to me that really both of these movements... if you read Irenaeus' description of this, Irenaeus is interesting because he clearly describes first of all this kind of Barbeloite theology, but notice that there, it's already christianised because the figure of Christ appears and then also he goes on to discuss next the interpretation of Genesis 2 through 9 that was later attributed to Ophites, and it's clear that that system also is christianised, because one of the members of the supreme Pentad is in fact Christ, who was considered to be the elder brother of Sophia, but again the real worker through most of that is the figure of Sophia. And as in the *Apocryphon of John*, she then becomes responsible for the origin of the world Creator Yaldabaoth, trouble breaks out and then the story reads very much as we find it in the *Apocryphon of John*. But then the damage that's been done is ultimately rectified by Sophia acting in concert with Christ, whereas in the barbeloite system, actually Sophia's mistake has to be undone by this higher mother figure called Barbelo.

MC: I think the one thing that we're missing, and as you write in your essays, is this group of priests who left the Temple, they must have run into some neo-Pythagoreans or Platonists, isn't that correct?

JT: Most literate Jews, I would think, certainly throughout the first century BCE and onwards, were, I think, well aware, at least in a popular sense, of the Platonic and the Pythagorean traditions. You know, Pythagoreanism is an interesting case in itself, because of course we find that early on, even in the early academy, that Plato was thought to have been well-versed in Pythagorean doctrines and so forth. Some of his earliest colleagues, people like Architos, were Pythagoreans, but as history goes on, in the platonic academy there was ultimately a reaction against this. They felt that Plato had become a kind of dogmatic metaphysician, especially in his later dialogues and in his so-called oral teaching, and that therefore he had ultimately been untrue to the teaching of Socrates, who himself is never represented as speculating about transcendent principles and so forth So, by and large, they rejected this transcendental metaphysics of Plato, and this then was the so-called Sceptical or New Academy. But then, interestingly, somewhere around the first century BCE, all of a sudden this kind of Platonic metaphysical speculation about ultimate principles and the one and the diad, and so forth, suddenly re-emerges under the name of Pythagoras, and so, in a very interesting way, Plato's very highest metaphysical teaching becomes claimed for Pythagoras. And this is the birth of Neo-Pythagoreanism

MC: And in their system, wasn't the Monad the supreme being? Did the Sethians borrow from that? Or call the Supreme Being the Monad? Or is he always the invisible spirit?

JT: No, actually it's interesting, right at the very beginning of the *Apocryphon of John* there's the suggestion that the supreme Invisible Spirit is a monarchy, is a monad, and the idea of course is the metaphysical problem—all these people try to deal with is—

how can the many come from the One? And this is the problem that neo-Pythagoreanism focussed upon. In some sense they took it almost as an axiom that somehow the ultimate essence of the world must be simpler than we perceive it to be. And therefore all things must have come from some one thing—it's almost a kind of analogy of certain speculations about the Big Bang theory—and so they then began to speculate along these kinds of numerical lines that somehow the One, by some mysterious process which is never successfully explained, gives rise to the Two. And then the One and the Two interact to produce the Three and then you have the possibility of a dimensional world and then finally you get, finally, a Four. And then a Four seems to be appropriate for discussing a three-dimensional world, and that represents the world that we can touch, taste and feel. And so, it comes by the interaction of these principles, which are given names for these primary numbers, the One, the Two, the Three and the Four which add up to ten, that is essentially the Pythagorean Tetract, as they called it, but the sacred Decad, find that it's reflected to a certain extent in the Gnostic treatises themselves, more especially, I would say, in Valentinian treatises where it's quite clear that the whole description of the transcendent world operates in terms of ones and twos and fours and that these combine together in ways to produce certain numerical groupings. So this is why it spread. In fact, one of the documents in the news recently, the *Gospel of Judas*—which is quite interesting—itself contains a kind of sketch of the Sethian theogeny or story of the birth and the development of the divine world and its gods. And it engages in a tremendous amount of numerical speculation, which, interestingly, seems to be quite clearly reflected in another of the Nag Hammadi documents, of which we have two copies in Nag Hammadi, called *Eugnostos the Blessed*, and it talks about the various pairings of these, and groups of four and groups of six, ultimately become 72 and this is then multiplied by five to become 360 which is the number of the year, the days in the year minus the five intercalary days and so forth...

MC: Frankly, one of the questions I wanted to ask you because Irenaeus says the *Gospel of Judas* was written by the Cainites but, even as you've just said, it seems much more of a Sethian work. Is there a connection between the Cainites or the Sethians, or could we possibly be talking

about two different *Gospels of Judas*?

JT: Boy, that's a complicated question! So, I'll say 'No' and 'Yes'.

MC: [laughs]

JT: No, in the sense that I don't think there was ever any group of Cainites. Irenaeus' text itself never names any people called Cainites, this was the name that was again added later by his epitomators, people like pseudo-Tertullian and Epiphanius and Theodoret and now we're getting, what, quite late into the fourth century. Whereas Irenaeus of course is a figure of the end of the second century, who never knew these names. I don't think that Irenaeus knew anything about Barbeloites or Sethians or Ophites or Cainites. But at the same time there is something tantalising here, you see, all Irenaeus mentions are Gnostics, first the 'multitude of Gnostics', who are the people who exhibit this, what I'm trying to characterise as a *Barbeloite* theology basically. Then he goes on to discuss these people who have a kind of supreme pentad who became later called Ophites, and who concentrate on, or are basically fascinated by the paradise story and all of that, which seems to be concentrated around the creation of the first human, his struggle to become enlightened, and that's in chapter 30. Then finally in chapter 31, there's this other group and it's in that context that he mentions this *Gospel of Judas* but he doesn't call these people Cainites...

MC: Uh-huh!

JT: ...of course Cain is mentioned as being a kind of an anti-hero along with the Sodomites and Cora and other sort of rebellious figures, but then he says that these people are utilising a certain *Gospel of Judas* but then he goes on to suggest that Judas of course was an especially enlightened figure, and that through his acts that he ended up then throwing the whole world into confusion. Well that doesn't really tell us very much. But then when you come on then to the later epitomators, people like Pseudo Tertullian probably in the early third century, Epiphanius and Theodoret in the fourth, suddenly we learn a lot more about this and they're concentrating on this notion that somehow Judas is the one whom we really ought to *thank,* because he ensured then the handing over of Jesus, which resulted in the supreme act of salvation for the church. Well of course *that* idea does *not* show up in the *Gospel of Judas* in spite of what its original editors have said about it. My own sense is that the preliminary version we all have is a kind of colossal misreading of that document itself...

MC: ah-hah!

JT: ..which I won't get into but it's certainly true that in the version that we have, yes indeed, Judas is an especially enlightened figure, but unfortunately he is a mere dupe of the stars, and so when he hands Jesus over, it's not at all because Jesus *asks* him to do this in such a way that therefore Judas can help effect this kind of sacrificial act of salvation through Jesus, but it's merely that he is a victim. He is predestined by the stars to do this, and Jesus merely predicts that that is what Judas is going to do. Quite clearly then, something is amiss and, coupled of course with the fact that once you pick up of course the *Gospel of Judas* and you get on down to page 51, suddenly you get this very, very long Sethian theogeny.

MC: Very true

JT: Which ends with the creation of the human being, but then oddly enough it's rather completely unlike the *Apocryphon of John* in its similar story, the story of paradise, because suddenly although our figures like Saklas and Yaldabaoth become as it were the evil creators of the world, suddenly there's no more attention to the paradise story and the place of the creation and once Eve and Adam are created, that's it—that's the end of it, and there's no account of the long series of moves and counter moves between the divine world and the evil creator Yaldabaoth. It's odd because if you compare it to the *Apocryphon of John*, much of the material in the second half of the *Apocryphon of John* which has to deal with that fascinating story of moves and counter moves between the transcendent world and this world is missing. It's not there at all and so, yes, it's clear therefore that we have

a kind of Sethian story here in the second part of the *Gospel of Judas* but it just, as it were, ends once the world has been brought into being and the primal pair arises, and at that point the Sethian material stops. So, my own sense is that we're dealing with a document that must have existed in several forms, one form probably known to Irenaeus, and another form according to the text that we possess today, but I don't think that they were necessarily one and the same document.

MC: Most of the readers already understand that there were three forms of people, the hylics, the psychics and the pneumatics. Do you see in Sethian literature some sort of similarity to that? Did the Sethians think that they were the perfected race?

JT: Yes, yes, they did. In fact the reason why it's legitimate to call them Sethians is because it does seem that they actually did have a self-designation, unlike most other Gnostic sects For example, Valentinians never called themselves Valentinians.

MC: Just Christians.

JT: Just called themselves Christians, and certainly the Sethians I don't think called themselves Sethians, but they did call themselves the Seed of Seth, they also thought of themselves as somehow victims of a kind of hostile world system, and by comparison, to most people they thought of themselves as rather pure, that is, they certainly have a tendency towards asceticism and so the most frequent self-designation seems to be the Worthy. They call themselves the Worthy, but certainly the Seed of Seth is a fairly distinctive self-designation. Now then when you come to the question you raised, Miguel, about this tripartite division of humanity into the pneumatics—the especially enlightened, perhaps enlightened, even saved by nature—and the psychic people, that is, in some sense, people who are on the way to gnosis but nevertheless had to engage in the struggle for purity and so forth—these are really the people in some sense to be saved—and then, finally, the hylics or the material people, who are beyond the pale and will be excluded.

This seems to be a product especially of the Valentinian schools, mainly—it may have originated actually with Valentinus' successor, Ptolemy—and the way in which he tried to approach these questions, but you don't see much evidence of that in Heracleon and certainly in Sethianism as far I can see. No evidence that they carved humanity up into these categories. If you read the *Apocryphon of John,* it becomes quite clear, towards the middle of the *Apocryphon of John* there's a kind of question and answer dialogue between Jesus and John, the son of Zebedee, where John asks Jesus a series of questions about the salvation of souls, and it turns out that there's only one class of people that is beyond the pale, and that's the people who grasp the truth and then rejected it, the turncoats, the apostates. So I would suggest that in some sense that the Sethians do not seem to have made this kind of general distinction. I would gather that in some sense everyone has this possibility for salvation, that what they need to do is of course to be awakened, so that they can get a much better grip on life and assess their position in the world. And then of course in the Sethian corpus, I mean, it's a rather large corpus, you've got fourteen original Gnostic treatises. For example, you've mentioned already the Granddaddy, the *Apocryphon of John* but to this we have to add the present version of the *Gospel of Judas* that we have, but then of course there's a number of reports on the part of heresiologists. We discussed of course mostly Irenaeus but we see this in the people who later copied Irenaeus, and even more information from, in the fourth century, from the church father Epiphanius. So, we have then, as it were, a lot of versions of the Sethian story, and one of the interesting things is that happened of course is… If I can back up a minute, I talked about my speculations of this arising in some kind of Jewish priestly environment, but then it's quite clear it then becomes Sethianised, that is, the figure of Seth somehow becomes important, and we don't know exactly where this come in, but I think it probably arose in some polemical context,

either with other Christians or, possibly, with other Jewish exegetes of the Book of Genesis. You know one of the refrains in the *Apocryphon of John* is, 'it is not as Moses said', says Christ 'but it is as I now tell you.'

MC: Right

JT: And one thing, one really begins to wonder, well, how does the figure of Seth come into all this? Well, Seth is an interesting figure in some other contexts for example, Josephus' *Antiquities* mentions for example that Seth played a special role in preserving primordial knowledge, the primordial knowledge of the arts of civilisation, by inscribing them on stone and brick steles, and we see this also in another interesting work—which has nothing, really, to do with Gnosticism—called the *Life of Adam and Eve,* which exists in several versions, Armenian and Latin and so forth…

MC: Really, never heard of it.

JT: Yes, right, a very interesting work, and in fact you can consult it on the web, just look for the *Life of Adam and Eve,* I think it's maybe Michael Stone who has put together an interesting collection of the various variants of that text. But I think that is possibly the key: why 'not as Moses said', because Moses wrote the Book of Genesis and it's *his* story about paradise but Moses was never *in* Paradise. Who *was* in paradise? *Adam* was in paradise.

MC: Right.

JT: Seth was in paradise and therefore, for example in the Sethian treatise of the *Apocalypse of Adam,* there we have it, right from the horse's mouth!

MC: [laughs].

JT: Right? Adam reveals to his son Seth what really *did* happen in paradise, and the assumption is there, what, Moses came later, right, he was the one who became the devotee of the god who revealed himself in the burning bush and gave the law on Sinai and so if you really want to know the *true* dope about what happened first..!

MC: [laughs].

JT: ...then you should consult Adam and Seth and I think that's ultimately how the figure of Seth became very important for the Sethians and Seth, since according to Genesis 4 and 5, he is the other seed that was born in the place of Cain, who had killed Abel. That and the priestly genealogy in Genesis 5 connects stuff directly with Adam. What's unique about Seth that, unlike anybody else, he was born in the image of his father, Adam, but then we of course know that Adam was born in the image of God!

MC: [laughs]Aha!

JT: That means Seth is another image of God. Which again gives it a certain special authority and so through observations of this sort, that's what attracts an interest in the figure of Seth. And then this Sethian tradition becomes christianised, especially, I think, throughout the second century although problems begin to break out towards the end of the second century, that Seth becomes identified with Christ where he is regarded as appearing on earth in the guise of Jesus. And two very interesting documents in this regard would be the *Trimorphic Protennoia*—for example, where protennoia descends in some sense to save Jesus from the cross—or even more, in the *Gospel of the Egyptian* where it's precisely Seth who is recognised as the one who puts on the body of Jesus and descends to overthrow the hostile archon. And in the literature it may be that the original name was Naamah or something like that, which means beautiful, but this clearly is the figure of Norea, who is understood as the wife/sister of Seth, although occasionally you find other identifications as well. One of the Sethian treatises in the Nag Hammadi is named *Norea* and she also becomes a prominent character in a problematic document in Codex II, where the *Apocryphon of John* is found, there is also a work called the *Hypostasis of the Archons* which is thought to be a Sethian document but is only obliquely Sethianised. Mainly because one of the revealer figures who comes to the aid of humans at the time of the flood is the angel Eleleth, who is the traditional fourth of the luminaries, but nevertheless Norea in some way tries to oppose the archon. The archon has a stratagem that he's going to use to save the race of humans by having Noah build the Ark, but Norea knows that this is a trick, that if the humans survive the flood, why then, Yaldabaoth will still be around and will still enslave people, so she tries to burn the Ark up but then the archons set upon her and she cries out for help to the angel Eleleth, so it's interesting there that it's not then at all Seth who is the Saviour figure in this document even though Hans-Martin Schenke who developed the original hypothesis of Sethianism thought that the *Hypostasis* would be a Sethian work, but it's actually Norea not Seth who becomes the kind of spokesman for Gnostic enlightenment.

MC: Another question which I thought was interesting is: Marvin Meyer in the *Gnostic Bible* puts *Thunder the perfect Mind* as a Sethian work-what is your stance on this?

JT: I'm not so sure. This is not his idea, of course, it was developed by Bentley Layton back around 1984, who wrote a very interesting article called 'The Riddle of the Thunder' mainly on the basis of certain testimonies we find in Irenaeus' treasure-chest

There, Epiphanius mentions a certain *Gospel of Eve*, and there's a statement attributed there that sounds very much like the sort of thing that you get—especially in the first paragraphs of the work, the *Thunder*—the same kind of riddling that we find on the occasion of the creation of Eve in two works in Nag Hammadi Codex II, the one I've just mentioned *The Hypostasis of the Archon*, but also In a sister work to that which has very few traces of Sethian theology, and it's called, though it actually has no title in Codex II, but we call it *On the Origin of the World*. Layton's solution is of course that the thunder is to be identified with Eve, but in that sense, she could be identified with almost any of these figures such as Norea, and so on

MC: or even Isis?

JT: Sure! And of course mainly on the grounds of the first- person self-predicatory statements, very typical of Isis. But it reads something like this:'I am the members of my mother, It is *I* who am the mother and the daughter, the wife and the virgin, I who am the barren, I who have many children, it is I who am the one whose marriage is magnificent and who is not married, it is I who am the midwife and she who does not give birth', these kind of antithetical self-predications. Well then you go on to the *Origin of the World*, and you see the story, as follows, where it says then that Eve is the first virgin who gave birth to her first offspring without a husband; it is she who served as her own midwife and so for this reason she is *held* to have said; 'It is I who am the member of my mother, I who am the wife and the virgin, I who am pregnant, I who am the midwife, I who am consolation of travail', and so forth.

And then in the *Hypostasis of the Archons* which comes then immediately before this thing we call *On The Origin of the World*, it says; 'The spirit endowed woman came to him and said 'Arise up!' When he saw her he said, 'It is you who have given me life, you who will be called Mother of the Living, for it is she who is my mother, she who is the midwife and she who has given birth."

MC: So that's how they got the connection!

JT: Sure, and so you know it was originally Layton who worked this over, and so in this case Marvin Myers adopted Layton's ideas.

MC: What other text would you recommend for someone who's interested in Sethian literature to read?

JT: I would always suggest maybe beginning with the *Apocryphon of John* and I've already mentioned two others in the course of our discussion, *The Hypostasis of the Archons*, a little tiny section of which I've just quoted. And then another very interesting one: *The Sacred Book of the Great Invisible Spirit*, which is popularly known as the *Gospel of the Egyptians*. 'The Gospel of the Egyptians' occurs in the colophon but that's not actually the title of the work, but the title of the work features the Great Invisible Spirit, the deity. But this is very interesting because it tells a lot about the Sethian ritual, a long section, clearly baptism but also there are

other acts, such as anointings, certain kinds of symbolic gestures made with ones hands to illustrate the vision of the divine world and the reception of light. I think I also mentioned briefly *The apocalypse of Adam* when I was talking about why Seth came to play a role in Sethian Gnosticism

MC: Uh-huh

JT: And this whole tradition about the steles or tablets or pillars of Seth that we see in Josephus and *The lives of Adam and Eve,* and we have a treatise called the *Three Steles of Seth* that comes at the very end of Codex VII. And then the Grand-Daddy of the Sethian works, the longest work in the Nag Hammadi library, is by the name of *Zostrianos*. And then there are others, the shortest of all called *The Thought of Norea* in Codex IX, *Melchizedek*, which unfortunately is very, highly fragmentary, nevertheless a very interesting text in which it seems that Jesus Christ and Melchisadek are somehow identified with one another as enlighteners, and that's also in Codex IX. But the thing that I've worked on most recently has been the connection between Sethianism and Greek philosophy which comes out primarily in *The Three Steles of Seth* , the long work *Zostrianus,* another very interesting work, the *Allogenes*, which seems to me to be the first evidence in western history of the doctrine of learned ignorance. This is mystical experience, so that one becomes ultimately to understand the highest deity by *not* knowing him. And then of course the treatise the *Trimorphic Protennoia* that comes from the thirteenth codex, although it was originally tucked in the inside front cover of Codex VI, that it once was a complete codex of itself. But the *Trimorphic Protennoia* (that is, 'The First Three-Formed Thought of God') is interesting because it too is very much like the *Thunder* because it's full of first-person self-predications of the divine Mother, who here is called Barbelo, she's called the First Thought of the High Deity and it has an amazing similarity to the conclusion of the *Apocryphon of John*, a kind of poetic triptych, a monologue of the divine protennoia, the first thought of Barbelo that occurs right at the end of the *Apocryphon* *of John*. The *Trimorphic Protennoia* seems to be a kind of an expansion of that. But anyway back to these ones that I mentioned, which I conceive to be the latest, that is, at some point, towards the end of the second century the turn of the third, this kind of loose alliance between the Sethians and the Christians fell apart mainly because the two became engaged in polemics. I think that Christians and the sort of apostolic churches came increasingly to object to this kind of identification between Christ and Seth. For the Sethians it was a natural identification, because Paul thinks of Christ as being in the image of God, Sethians think of Seth as being in the image of God , so clearly they're both images of God and so, in some sense they must be inter-identifiable. But there were Christian theologians who, obviously objected to this kind of thing. And so I think that is what happened.

The first-century theologian Victorinus and the treatise *Zostrianus* share word-for-word a common source, which has raised a very interesting question in the history of Greek philosophy that centres around the question: what was the origin of the theological interpretation of Plato's *Parmenides*? I'm sure you've seen references to the idea of negative theology—this you encounter almost at the very beginning of the *Apocryphon of John*.

MC: Yeah.

JT: Traditionally we connect it with the second half of Plato's *Parmenides* which then goes on to discuss the problem of unity and of otherness in terms of these eight hypotheses, and the first one therefore is the consideration of the one so pure that you can't even attribute being to it, and so on. Well, it's clear this has made an impact in these negative theologies, and we see them in the Sethian treatises, and, my sense is that quite possibly it was the Gnostics who, even before Plotinus, they have been instrumental in instituting this kind of religious, theological interpretation of the *Parmenides*, which before their time was regarded as a kind of logical exercise in dialectic. So, I mean, in various ways, these treatises, prove to be enlightening not only for the history of religion but also for the

history of Greek philosophy I wrote my book about called *Sethian Gnosticism and the Platonic Tradition*.

MC: Thank you much, John.

JT: Happy to discuss it at any time

John Turner

The Three Steles of Seth

The Three Steles of Seth from Nag Hammadi Codex VII, 5: 118,10-127:27:

I. Introduction: Dositheus' Vision of the Steles

Dositheus' revelation of of the three steles of Seth, the father of the living and unshakeable race. He saw and understood them. After he read them, he remembered them and delivered them to those chosen ones, just as they were written there.Many times I joined in glorifying along with the powers, and I was deemed worthy by the immeasurable Magnitudes.

Now they are as follows:

THE FIRST STELE OF SETH

II. Hymns to Pigeradamas, Autogenes, the Barbelo Aeon, and the Supreme One

Hymn 1: Emmakha Seth praises Pigeradamas

I bless you, O father Pigeradamas, I, your own son Emmacha Seth, whom you generated without procreation for the praise of our god.

For I am your own son.

And it is you who are my intellect, my father. Now, I for my part have sown and procreated while you, for your part, have beheld the Magnitudes and have ceaselessly stood at rest .

I bless you, [O] Father; bless me, O Father. It is because of you that I exist; it is because of God that you exist. Because of you I exist in the presence of that very one.

You are light, beholding light; you have shown forth light. You are a Mirotheid (offspring of Mirothea); it is you who are my Mirotheos.I bless you as a deity, I bless your divinity:

Hymn 2: Emmakha Seth Praises Autogenes

Great is the good Autogenes who stood at rest, the God who first stood at rest! You came with goodness, you appeared, and you manifested goodness.

I shall utter your name: for you are a prime name. You are unengendered: for your part, you have appeared

that you might show forth
those that are eternal.
It is you who are the one that is; therefore
you manifested those that truly exist.
It is you who are spoken of by voice,
but by intellect you are glorified .
It is you who are powerful everywhere.
Therefore because of you and your seed
even [the] perceptible universe knows you:
you are merciful.

 And you derive from another kind (i.e.,
the primal triad) and it presides over
another kind (i.e., the Barbelo Aeon).
But now, you derive from another
kind, and it presides over another
kind (i.e., the seed of Seth).
You derive from another kind, for you
are [dissimilar] (i.e., to other humans).
And you are merciful,
 for you are eternal.

It is over a kind that you preside,
 for you have caused all these (i.e.,
the spiritual 'seed') to increase.
And (you did this) for the sake of my seed,
 for it is you who know that it resides
in (the realms of) procreation.
And they derive from another kind,
 for they are dissimilar (i.e.,
to other humans).
And they reside above other
kinds (i.e., other humans),
 for they reside in life.

You are a Mirotheos (perhaps 'divine
anointed one' myro+theos)! I praise its
power, which has been given unto me.

**Hymn 3: Collective Hymn in Praise
of the Barbelo Aeon as Triple Male**

O you who have caused the truly existent
masculinities to be Triple Male!

O you who have been divided
into the pentad!
O you who have been given
to us in triple power!
O you who have been
ingenerately generated!
O you who came forth from the superior
and for the sake of the inferior
have gone forth into (or: from) the middle!
You are a father issued from a father,
a word issued from a command.
We praise you, O Triple Male, for you
have unified the All from them all,
 for you have empowered us.
From Unity you originated;through
Unity you came forth;into
Unity you have entered.

[You] have saved, you have
saved, you have saved us!
O crown-bearer, O crown-bestower,
we praise you eternally.
We praise you, we who have been
saved as the perfect individuals,
perfect because of you, [having
become] perfect along with you.

O perfect one! O perfecter!
The one who is complete through all these!
The one who is everywhere similar!
O Triple Male!

You have stood at rest; you
were first to stand at rest.
You have become divided everywhere,
and you have remained One.And
whomever you willed, you saved,

and all those who are worthy,
you will to be saved.
You are perfect! You are
perfect! You are perfect!

The First Stele of Seth
THE SECOND STELE OF SETH

Hymn 4: Collective Praise to the Barbelo Aeon as Unified Author of Multiplicity

Great is the first, masculine,
virginal Aeon of Barbelo,
the first glory of the invisible Father!
O you (sg.) who are called perfect,
you yourself first saw that the one who
truly pre-existents is non-being,
and from it and through it you
have eternally proceeded.
O non-being One from an undivided
Triple [Powered] One,
You are a triple power!

You are [a] great monad
from [a] pure monad!
You are a superior monad,
the first [projection (shadow)] of
the holy Father, light from light!

[We] bless you, O generator of
perfection and supplier of aeons!
You yourself have [seen]
that the eternal ones
derive from a projection (shadow).

And you have given rise to multiplicity:
Yet you turned out to remain One,
even though by giving rise to
multiplicity through division
you are threefold. Truly you are threefold!

You are One (fem.) belonging
to the One (masc.),
and you derive from its projection.
You are a Kalyptos (hidden one)!You are
a universe of understanding,knowing
that those belonging to the One
derive from a projection (shadow).
And these are yours in thought.

For their sake you have empowered the
eternal ones by Substantiality;you have
empowereddivinity by Vitality; you have
empowered Mentality by goodness.

By Blessedness you have empowered
the projections flowing from the One.
By Mentality you have empowered
one; By Quality (txt: 'creation')
you have empowered another;
You have empowered the equal and
unequal, the similar and the dissimilar.
With generation and intelligible forms
you have empowered others in Being
[to flourish] with generation.
You have empowered these—this is
Kalyptos (hidden one)— by thought,
and you [have] emanated unto
these and [out of] these.
You are divided among them, and you
become a great male Intellect, Protophanes.

O paternal God! Divine child!
Generator of multiplicity!
By division of all those that truly
existyou have appeared to them all
as a Word (i.e., Autogenes?).
And you possess them all ingenerately,
eternally, imperishably.

Hymn 5: Collective Invocation and Petition to the Barbelo Aeon to Enable the Ascent

Because of you salvation has come to us;
from you comes salvation!

You are wisdom (Sophia)! You are
knowledge! You are truth!

Because of you is Life; from you
comes Life.Because of you is Intellect;
from you comes Intellect.
You are Intellect; you are
a universe of truth.
You are a triple power; you are threefold!
Truly, you are triple, O Aeon of aeons!
It is you alone who see purely the
eternal and unengendered primal
principles,but also the primal divisions,
according as you have been divided.

Unify us according as you have
been unified!Teach us [about] the
things you see!Empower us, that we
might be saved to eternal life.
For, as for us, we are a projection
(shadow) of you,
[just] as you are a projection (shadow)
of the one that primally preexists.

Hear us first—we are eternal!
Hear us—the perfect individuals!
It is you who are the aeon of aeons,
the all-perfect One who is unified.
Thanksgiving to the Barbelo
Aeon for enabling the Ascent
You have heard! You have heard!

You have saved! You have saved!We
give thanks! We bless you

always! We will glorify you!
The Second Stele of Seth

THE THIRD STELE

Hymn 6: Collective Praise and Petition to the Supreme One

We rejoice! We rejoice ! We rejoice!

We have seen! We have seen! We have
seen the one that truly preexists,who truly
exists, who is the eternal first principle!

O unengendered one, from you come
the eternal ones, even the aeons,
the All-perfect who are unified,
and the Perfect individuals!

We bless you, O non-being Existence
prior to existences,first Being prior
to beings, Father of Divinity and
Vitality,creator of Intellect, bestower
of Good, bestower of Blessedness!
We all bless you, O knower,
with [glorificatory] praise,
the one on whose account all [these are].

[It is you who knows those
who truly] [exist],
O you who know yourself
through yourself alone!
For there is nothing that is
active prior to you.

You are spirit, alone and living.
And [you] know Unity, the Unity that
is yours of which we cannot speak.
Indeed your light is shining upon us.
Command us to see you, so
that we might be saved!

It is knowledge of you that is the salvation of us all.Command! If you command, we have been saved!
Hymn: Collective Thanksgiving to the Supreme One
Truly we have been saved!

We have seen you by means of Intellect. You are all of these, for you save them all, you whoneither shall be saved nor have been saved by them.For, as for you, you have commanded us.
You are One, you are One!
Just as one would say of you
that you are One,
you are a single, living spirit.How shall we name you? It is not ours to say!For you are the Existence of them all;you are the Life of them all;
you are the Intellect of them all.
[For it is] you in whom [they] all rejoice.
It is you who have commanded them all to [be saved]
by your [word to the extent that] they [are able].
O [first Glory] before him, [O] Kalyptos (hidden one),
blessed Senaon, [self-]generated one!
[Asi]neus! Mephneus! Optaon !
Elemaon the great power!
Emouniar! Nibareus! Kandephoros!
Aphredon! Deiphaneus!

You who are Armedon for me,
O generator of powers:
Thalanatheus! Antitheus!It is you who exist within yourself,
you who are before yourself,
and after you none came into activity.
With what shall we bless you? We

cannot!But as inferiors we give thanks to you,for you as the superior have commanded us to glorify you
to the extent that we are able.
We praise you since we have been saved; we glorify you constantly!
Now we glorify you that we might be saved to eternal salvation.We have blessed you, for we are able.
We have been saved, for you have always desired thatwe all do so, and we all did so.[We will] not [do it] through [...] [...] [...] [...], who has [...],
we together with those who [have been saved].

III. Dositheus' Directions for using the Hymn during the Mystical Ascent

Whoever remembers these and always glorifies shall become perfect among the perfect and impassive beyond all things. For they all bless these individually and collectively, and afterward they shall be silent. And just as they were ordained, they ascend. After the silence, they descend from the third; they bless the second; and after these, the first. The path of ascent is the path of descent. Know then, as those who live, that you have arrived and have taught yourselves about the infinites. Marvel at the truth that is within them, and the revelation!

IV. Concluding Scribal Benediction

This book belongs to the fatherhood. It is the son who wrote it.Bless me, O Father. I bless you, O Father, in peace. Amen!

William S. Burroughs by John Coulthart

Sven Davisson

Burroughs-ian Gnosticism
In His Own Words

Burroughs explicitly linked his philosophy to Manichaeism—a third century Persian religion. Manichaeism was founded by a young preacher, Mani in the early to mid third century of the Common Era. Mani was heavily influenced by Gnostic Christianity—calling himself a 'disciple of Christ' and the 'Paraclete,' or biblical healer. The Manichaens incorporated many existing belief systems into their world-view. From Mandeanism and Gnosticism, they appropriated a strongly held belief in cosmic dualism. It is in this sense that Burroughs links his philosophy to that of the third century religion. Burroughs' fiction and nonfiction work (as the two are not readily separable) are best characterized as mythology. He himself described his effort as writing a mythology for the space age. His philosophy has many parallels to early Gnosticism that go beyond this simple invocation of Manichaeism dualism.

Burroughs first encountered the concept of the Johnson Family while still a boy reading the book *You Can't Win* by Jack Black. First published in the 1920's Black's autobiographical account of hobo life was immensely popular in its day. Burroughs describes the Johnsons in *The Place of Dead Roads*:

'The Johnson Family' was a turn-of-the-century expression to designate good bums and thieves. It was elaborated into a code of conduct. A Johnson honors his obligations. His word is good and he is a good man to do business with. A Johnson minds his own business. He is not a snoopy, self-righteous, trouble-making person. A Johnson will give help when help is needed. He will not stand by while someone is drowning or trapped under a burning car.[2]

In his essay 'The Johnson Family,' Burroughs elaborates on the Johnsons' philosophical placement within his mythic system—explicitly linking them to Manichaeistic dualism:

The Johnson family formulates a Manachean position where good and evil are in conflict and the outcome is at this point uncertain. It is *not* an eternal conflict since one or the other must win a final victory.[3]

In contrast to the honorable world of hobos and criminals, Burroughs describes a type of person known simply as a 'Shit.' Unlike the Johnsons, Shits are obsessed with minding other's business. They are the town busy body, the preacher, the lawman. Shits are incapable of taking the honorable road of each-to-his-own. Burroughs describes the situation in his essay 'My Own Business' thus:

This world would be a pretty easy and pleasant place to live in if everybody could just mind his own business and let others do the same. But a wise old black faggot said to me years ago: 'Some people are shits, darling.' I was never able to forget it.[4]

In Burroughs' mythology, the world is one of conflict between the Johnsons and the Shits. A Shit is one who is obsessively sure of his own position at the cost of all other vantages. Burroughs describes Shits as incapable of minding 'their own business, because they have no business of their own to mind, any more than a small pox virus has.'[5] This is more than an offhanded analogy. For Burroughs, Shits are, in actuality, virus occupied hosts—chronically infected by what he terms the Right virus. 'The mark of a basic Shit,' Burroughs reminds us, 'is that he has to be *right*.'[6]

The war between the Johnsons and the Shits is epic and runs throughout Burroughs' writing. Though of immense proportions, like the Gnostic battle between good and evil, the cosmic war is not figured across eternity. It has an end and, for Burroughs, that end is imaginable. It does not come without immense conflict, however. Burroughs tells his reader, 'The people in power will not disappear voluntarily.'[7] There is no turning back, once the battle is met. 'Once you take up arms against a bunch of shits there is no way back. Lay down your arms and they will kill you.'[8] 'Hell hath no more vociferous fury than an endangered parasite.'[9] But remember, also: 'The wild boys take no prisoners.'[10]

In discussing his mythology, Burroughs describes a classic Catch-22: 'He who opposes force with counterforce alone forms that which he opposes and is formed by it... On the other hand he who does not resist force that enslaves and exterminates will be enslaved and exterminated.'[11] Burroughs' work begs the question, how does one resist the forces rallied against one without taking on the viral-taint of that opposing force. To imagine a permanent solution proves an all too easy flirtation. In his essay 'My Own Business,' Burroughs writes that 'one is tempted to seek a total solution to the problem: Mass Assassination Day.'[12]

In *The Place of Dead Roads* Burroughs imagines a scenario where the Johnson Family organizes into armed squads that fan out to hunt those infected with the right virus. Some Johnsons are assigned as 'Shit Spotters' whose task it is to move out into cities and small towns across the country recording those who exhibit virus occupied behaviors. Acting upon the intelligence thus gathered, sharp shooters follow-up eliminating the detected Shits.[13] Ultimately Burroughs tempers his fantasy. He observes, 'Probably the most effective tactic is to alter the conditions on which the virus subsists.'[14]

In truth, indifference will prove the end of the Shit problem. 'Conditions change, and the virus guise is ignored and forgotten.'[15] Burroughs envisions the Shit position obsoleted by changes in normative culture:

> This trend toward sanity has brought the last-ditch dedicated shits out into the open, screaming with rage. Victimless crime, the assumption that what a citizen does in the privacy of his own dwelling is nonetheless someone else's business and therefore subject to denunciation and punishment is the very lifeline of the *right* virus. Cutting off this air line would have the same action as interferon, which blocks the oxygen from certain virus strains.[16]

And slowly the Shits are ignored into a dull, dated celluloid sunset.

Like many of the early Gnostics, Burroughs believed that humanity was tainted from birth by outside elements. Within his writing, all humanity is infected from the outset. 'We are all tainted with viral origins.'[17] '[T]he whole quality of human consciousness, as expressed in male and female, is basically a viral mechanism.'[18] He posits a theory of 'inverse evolution.' Also like the early Gnostics, Burroughs cosmology contains a parallel to the Fall. He suggests that 'Man did not rise out of the animal state, he was shoved down to be an animal to be animals to be a body to be bodies by the infamous Fifth Columnists.'[19]

Due to this viral mechanism, the cosmic conflict is configured within the domain of our own bodies. Burroughs wonders if 'the separation of the sexes' isn't 'an arbitrary device to perpetuate an unworkable arrangement.'[20] Theorist Robin Lydenberg writes that Burroughs sees 'the only possible relationship between two sexes defined in binary opposition to each other is one of conflict.'[21] For Burroughs this arena of perpetual conflict, enacted through and on the zone of the body, is one of the largest elements standing between humanity and the potential to mutate into something with even the slightest chance of survival. In *The Wild Boys*, Burroughs writes, 'What holds me back? It is the bargain by which I am here at all. The bargain is this body that holds me here.'[22]

Lydenberg continues her analysis:

Burroughs attributes the polarization of reproductive energy to structures of binary opposition which set two incompatible sexes in perpetual conflict, channeling the flow of creative energy into a parasitic economy based on power and property.[23]

Burroughs suggests that this division has trapped humans in a state of neotany, arrested evolution (A.E.). He writes, 'I am advancing the theory that we were not designed to remain in our present state, any more than a tadpole is designed to remain a tadpole forever.'[24] Within his mythology, there is very little hope that humanity will make it out. The necessary mutation that might spur us back onto the evolutionary path may prove unattainable. Bleakly, he writes in *The Western Lands*:

Man is indeed the final product. Not because homo sap is the apogee of perfection, before which God himself gasps in awe—'I can do nothing more!'—but because Man is an unsuccessful experiment, caught in a biologic dead end and inexorably headed for extinction.[25]

And…

It is inconceivable that Homo sapiens could last another thousand years in present form.[26]

Burroughs did believe in reincarnation. In interviews, he described it as a 'given.' 'I have written [in *The Place of Dead Roads*], Kim had never doubted the existence of gods or the possibility of an after-life and Kim is my alter ego and spokesman like Larry Speaks.' Birth, however, 'is something to be avoided… the worst thing that could happen.'[27] For Burroughs, it seems, the real trick is not to be born in the first place. 'The human condition is hopeless once you submit to it by being born…*almost*. There is one chance in a million and that is still good biologic odds.'[28] *Almost*, and the slightest

glimmer creeps in.

As Burroughs sees it, the only escape possible for humanity is biologic mutation. This is nothing less than an evolutionary jump into the unknown—a complete and total movement away from what one knows as human. Burroughs writes in *The Western Lands*: 'A problem cannot be solved in terms of itself. The human problem cannot be solved in human terms.'[29] And in his essay 'Immortality' he warns us 'Mutation involves changes that are literally unimaginable from the perspective of the future mutant.'[30] The mutation he envisions represents 'A step into the unknown, a step that no human being has ever taken before.'[31] Once one takes the step there will be no turning back. 'Evolution would seem to be a one-way street.'[32]

The Gnostics believed that the world was created by an evil being, the Demiurge known as IALDABOATH. This being was an abortive creation of Sophia, the embodiment of cosmic wisdom, formed when she took creation unto herself without the knowledge of the non-dual prime-entity. The Demiurge is unaware of his own origin and thinks of himself as the one and only GOD of his creation. One finds strong parallels to this cosmology within Burroughs mythos. The world is actually at the mercy of an ephemeral, but all too real, force Burroughs calls simply 'Control.' In *The Western Lands* he writes, 'We are controlled by the Powers. Not one, but many, and often in conflict. It is all part of some Power Plan.'[33]

Burroughs views the modern period as characterized by an insidious display of Control's raw authority unprecedented in history. Within his fiction, he depicts a world of 'control madness,' which is predicated on the modern wholesale presentation of image and word, constructed through careful manipulation of the media, the state, religion and advertising. For Burroughs, the modern world is characterized by 'random elements' that have come to power through accidental conditions. Modern leaders are the 'unwitting' agents of control. Thus, 'the iron-willed dictator is a thing of the past.'[34]

In Burroughs' work the modern world is a horrific terrain of constructed knowledge—organically directed toward the eradication of all free thought. Contrasting this modern manifestation of Control with its historical antecedents, Burroughs writes, 'To confuse this old-style power with the manifestation of control madness we see now on this planet is to confuse a disappearing wart with an exploding cancer.'[35]

Just like humanity's precarious position in a state of neotany, Burroughs sees that the presence of Control is not perpetual. Again the cosmic conflict is not eternal. For Burroughs, humanity is in 'the last game.'[36] In *The Western Lands*, Burroughs writes of Control's ultimate plan:

> The program of the ruling elite in Orwell's *1984* was: 'A foot stamping on a human face forever!' This is naïve and optimistic. No species could survive for even a generation under such a program. This is not a program of eternal, or even long-range dominance. It is clearly an *extermination program*.[37]

Finally…

> The door closes behind you, and you begin to know where you are. This planet is a Death Camp… the Second and Final Death.[38]

Just like the evil God of the Gnostics, Burroughs' concept of Control masquerades as the axiomatic, natural laws of the Cosmos. In *The Job*, Burroughs notes, 'All control systems claim to reflect the immutable laws of the universe.'[39] Control wears the mask of religion, temporal law enforcement, the righteous politician. The greatest tactic of Control represented within Burroughs' work is that of the One God Universe (OGU):

> Consider the One God Universe: OGU. The spirit recoils in horror from such a deadly impasse. He is all-powerful and all-knowing. Because He can do everything, He can do nothing, since the act of doing demands opposition. He knows everything, so there is nothing for him to learn. He can't

go anywhere, since He is already fucking everywhere, like cowshit in Calcutta.

> The OGU is a pre-recorded universe of which He is the recorder. It's a flat, thermodynamic universe, since it has no friction by definition. So He invents friction and conflict, pain, fear, sickness, famine, war, old age and Death.[40]

Compare this One God with the Gnostic conception of the Demiurge.

For Burroughs, the notion of One God is simply a method employed by Control. It is akin to the Mayan calendar system in which each moment was predictable as it was pre-recorded. No matter the holy book or the messenger, the notion of One God proves little more than a palliative film shown to prisoners on Death Row. In such a system, resistance is a dangerous move:

> So the One God, backed by secular power, is forced on the masses in the name of Islam Christianity, the state, for all secular leaders want to be the One. To be intelligent or observant under such a blanket of oppression is to be 'subversive.'[41]

While describing his concept of the One God Universe, Burroughs outlines his contrasting view of a Magical Universe. 'The most basic concept of my writing,' he writes, 'is a belief in the magical universe, a universe of many gods, often in conflict. The paradox of an all-powerful, all-seeing God who nonetheless allows suffering, evil, and death, does not arise.'[42] Like the Gnostics, Burroughs held the belief that through contact with this magical universe, one could break free of the confines of the One God Universe, thus moving outside the grasp of Control. Burroughs image of the Garden of Alamout is analogous to the way the Gnostics employed the vision of the Kingdom. A glimpse of either is transformative—a Gnostic vision taking one above the realm of the evil creator god, the Demiurge or Control. For Burroughs, through dream visions, one becomes a god:

> You need your dreams, they are a biologic necessity and your lifeline to space, that is,

to the state of God. To be one of the Shining Ones. The inference is that Gods are a biologic necessity. They are an integral part of Man.[43]

Burroughs appropriates the Egyptian notion of an after life, a paradise known as 'The Western Lands.' Unlike the Christian or Islamic heavens, entry to the Western Lands is by no means guaranteed through actions within one's life. It does, in fact, lie at the end of a dangerous journey—one in which portions of the soul struggle to reach immortality. Burroughs asks his readers to compare his mythological description of the Western Lands with the shoddy images of paradise promised by the proponents of the One God Universe:

Look at their Western Lands. What do they look like? The houses and gardens of a rich man. Is this all the Gods can offer?[44]

Well, I say then it is time for new Gods who do not offer such paltry bribes. It is dangerous to think such things. It is very dangerous to live, my friend, and few survive it. And one does not survive by shunning danger, when we have a universe to win and absolutely nothing to lose. It is already lost.[45]

In *The Place of Dead Roads*, he tells us unequivocally: 'This is no vague eternal heaven for the righteous. This is an actual place at the end of a very dangerous road.'[46]

Burroughs sees that historically 'the Gods held all their keys and admitted only favored mortals.'[47] This was the case in the Egyptian system, described in their *Book of the Dead*, where gods and demons had to be placated, propitiated and answered with their sacred names throughout the nearly impossible journey across the wasteland between earthly life and the Western Lands. Like the Gnostics, Burroughs' mythology proposes, no matter how remotely, the possibility that one may discover the hidden key (gnosis) that opens the secret wisdom represented by the Western Lands. Again like the Gnostics, Burroughs understood that this metaphorical key unlocked not just one

revelation, but everything in an instant. This is the vision of the Kingdom conveyed by Jesus, or the Illuminator, in the Gnostic scriptures. Burroughs writes, 'Once you find the key, there are not just one garden but many gardens, an infinite number.'[48]

Throughout his own Book of the Dead, Burroughs frequently warns us of the treacherous nature of the journey:

The road to the Western Lands is by definition the most dangerous road in the world, for it is a journey beyond Death, beyond the basic God standard of Fear and Danger. It is the most heavily guarded road in the world, for it gives access to the gift that supersedes all other gifts: Immortality.[49]

And…

The Road to the Western Lands is devious, unpredictable. Today's easy passage may be tomorrow's death trap. The obvious road is almost always a fool's road, and beware the Middle Roads, the roads of moderation, common sense and careful planning. However, there is a time for planning, moderation and common sense.[50]

Within his mythology, Burroughs appears to suggest that the end is all but a given. The final trains are moving inexorably toward the gates of the camp. There are many ways in, but no exit. For humanity, stuck for millennia just moments before mutation, there seems no escape for the soul. No windows give sight of the future, but the smell of the charnel fires are a dead give-away. Perhaps it is too late and we have already moved past the evolutionary point of no-return—already dinosaurs in dénouement. But, with Burroughs, there is always an *almost*.

Burroughs' close friend and collaborator Brion Gysin reminds us: 'The outbreak of Armegeddon made things infinitely more complicated but all that much more urgent.'[51]

References:

Burroughs, William S. *Cities of the Red Night.* New York: Holt, Rinehart and Winston, 1981.

_____. 'Immortality,' in *The Adding Machine: Collected Essays.* London: John Calder Publishers, 1985, 127-136.

_____. *The Job.* New York: Penguin, 1974.

_____. 'The Johnson Family,' in *The Adding Machine: Collected Essays.* London: John Calder Publishers, 1985, 74-7.

_____. 'My Own Business,' in *The Adding Machine: Collected Essays.* London: John Calder Publishers, 1985, 15-8.

_____. 'My Purpose is to Write For the Space Age,' in *William S. Burroughs at the Front: Critical Reception, 1959-1989,* Jennie Skerl and Robin Lydenberg, eds. Carbondale, IL: Southern Illinois University Press, 1991.

_____. 'No more Stalins, no more Hitlers' on *Dead City Radio* (sound recording), New York: Island Records, 1990.

_____. *The Place of Dead Roads.* New York: Holt, Rinehart and Winston, 1983.

_____. *Port of Saints.* Berkeley, CA: Blue Wind Press, 1980.

_____. *The Western Lands.* New York: Penguin, 1987.

_____. *The Wild Boys: A Book of the Dead.* New York: Grove, 1978.

_____. 'Women: A Biological Mistake?' in *The Adding Machine: Collected Essays.* London: John Calder Publishers, 1985, 124-6.

Gysin, Brion. *The Last Museum.* New York: Grove, 1986.

Lydenberg, Robin. Word Cultures: Literary Form and Theory in the Radical Writings of William S. Burroughs. New York: Routledge, 1988.

Maeck, Klaus. *William S. Burroughs: Commissioner of Sewers.* New York: Mytic Fire Video, 1986.

Notes

1 Article previously published in *The Starry Dynamo: The Machinery of Night Remixed* (Rebel Satori Press, 2007)

2 *The Place of Dead Roads*, iv.

3 'The Johnson Family,' 75-76.

4 'My Own Business,' 15.

5 Ibid, 16.

6 Ibid, 16.

7 *The Job*, 74.

8 'The Johnson Family,' 77.

9 'My Own Business,' 16.

10 *The Wild Boys*, 148.

11 *The Job*, 100.

12 'My Own Business,' 17.

13 *The Place of Dead Roads*, 155-6.

14 'My Own Business,' 18.

15 Ibid, 18.

16 Ibid, 16.

17 *Cities of the Red Night*, 25.

18 Ibid, 25.

19 *Port of Saints*, 105.

20 'Women: A Biological Mistake?' 126.

21 Lydenberg, 162.

22 *The Wild Boys*, 103.

23 Lydenberg, 156.

24 'Women: A Bioloogical Mistake?' 125.

25 *The Western Lands*, 41.

26 Ibid, 223.

27 Maeck.

28 *The Western Lands*, 199.

29 *The Western Lands*, 27.

30 'Immortality,' 135.

31 Ibid, 135.

32 'Women: A Biological Mistake?' 125.

33 *The Western Lands*, 188.

34 'No more Stalins, no more Hitlers.'

35 *The Job*, 60.

36 *The Western Lands*, 254.

37 Ibid, 59.

38 Ibid, 254.

39 *The Job*, 43.

40 *The Western Lands*, 113.

41 Ibid, 111.

42 'My Purpose Is to Write for the Space Age,' 268.

43 *The Western Lands*, 181.

44 Ibid, 184.

45 Ibid, 184

46 *The Place of Dead* Roads, 171.

47 Ibid, 171.

48 Ibid, 171.

49 *The Western Lands*, 124.

50 Ibid, 151.

51 Gysin, 105.

Michael W. Grondin

No Man's Land: The Meyer-Patterson Family of Thomas Translations

Most English translations of the Gospel of Thomas in use today were published in the period 1987-1998, beginning with Bentley Layton's in *The Gnostic Scriptures* and culminating with the Patterson-Robinson adaptation in *The Fifth Gospel*. Of the translations published in this twelve-year period, the names of Marvin Meyer and Stephen Patterson feature prominently, being attached to a family of translations which they produced jointly (first group below) and singly:

Q-Thomas Reader, Kloppenborg, Meyer, Patterson, Steinhauser (1990)

The Five Gospels, Funk, Hoover, The Jesus Seminar (1993) - designated 'T5G'

The Complete Gospels, Miller, ed., (1992, 1994) - designated 'TCG'
The Gospel of Thomas: The Hidden Sayings of Jesus, Meyer, 1992

The Gospel of Thomas and Jesus, Patterson, 1993 (sayings unordered)

With the exception of Meyer 1992 (Harper-Collins), all of the above were published by Polebridge Press, which is associated with the Westar Institute and the Jesus Seminar, under the direction of Robert Funk. The versions that appear in T5G and TCG picked up the title 'Scholar's Version' because that was the general designation for *all* of the translations contained therein, in spite of the fact that the title properly applied only to canonical texts. As Funk explained it:

'The Scholars Version—SV for short—is free of ecclesiastical and religious control, unlike other major translations into English ...' (TCG, p.vii)

But the translations of *non-canonical* works like Thomas have *always* been produced by scholars who have been 'free of ecclesiastical and religious control', so the title 'Scholar's Version' is misleading when applied to those works. That doesn't stop it from functioning as a promotional device, however. (If you were working for PBS, say, and you had to choose between Thomas translations, wouldn't you pick the one that was called the 'Scholar's Version'?)

It should also be noted in passing that there are differences between the Thomas translations in T5G and TCG, such that one might well ask '*Which* Scholar's Version?' (PBS used TCG.) Most of the 22 differences in 13 sayings are minor, but in two places (sayings 35 and 63), TCG has 'man' where T5G has 'person'. This is remarkable because nowhere else does TCG have 'man', and T5G has it nowhere at all (which of course is my main concern in this essay). One would assume that TCG, being later than T5G, would be an updated and corrected version. But it seems not to be, for Meyer and Patterson haven't changed their minds that there is nowhere in the Gospel of Thomas where the words 'man' or 'men' should appear in an English translation. 'Woman' yes, but 'man' no. This is an extraordinary position which, as will be seen, is at striking variance not only with other Thomas translators, but even with their own fellows on the T5G/TCG translation panels. And there is no good reason for it.

To put the issue in context, bear in mind that the Coptic word for 'man' (rōme) occurs 35 times in the text. Meyer and Patterson translate that word usually as 'person', sometimes 'human being', etc., but never as 'man' or 'men'. In contrast, they never translate the Coptic word for 'woman' as 'person'. This policy contrasts rather markedly with other scholarly Thomas translations, such as those of Lambdin, Blatz, Layton, and DeConick, surveyed below.

The Thomas translation with the most authoritative pedigree is that of Thomas Lambdin, the author of *Introduction to Sahidic Coptic* (1982), the standard classroom textbook on the subject. Lambdin's revised Thomas translation (there had been an earlier one in 1977) was published in the 1988 edition of *The Nag Hammadi Library*, and subsequently appeared in Bentley Layton's two-volume critical edition of Nag Hammadi Codex II (1989). Properly ignoring a handful of superfluous occurrences of the Coptic word *rōme*, Lambdin translated 30 of them as 'man/men'. Similarly, the translation associated with the name of the German translator Beate Blatz in *New Testament Apocrypha* (1991), the standard work on apocryphal texts, contains 29 instances of 'man/men' in those places.

A third class of translations is the result of attempting to minimize gender-bias in Thomas, which shares the characteristic of other ancient writings of using 'man' in two senses: sometimes to refer to a male individual, sometimes to refer to humankind in general. Members of this class of translations would include the afore-mentioned Layton translation (1987) and one of the few recent English translations, that of April DeConick in *The Original Gospel of Thomas in Translation* (2006).

The surveyed translations fall into three general groups, based on the number of occurrences of *rōme* which are translated 'man/men', and employing some fanciful category-names:

'Manful': Lambdin (30), NTA-Blatz (29)

'Mansome': Layton (12), DeConick (15)

'Manless': Meyer and Patterson, jointly and singly

'Manful' translations are justified because they faithfully translate *rōme* as 'man'. 'Mansome' translations are justified because they attempt to distinguish the two senses of *rōme*. But what is the justification for 'Manless' translations? Three have been offered, either in print or in personal correspondence between myself and Professors Meyer and Patterson:

1. In print, Meyer and Patterson appeal only to gender neutrality, but if that's the rationale, the translational result is clearly over-kill. The elimination of gender bias isn't achieved by the deletion of every 'man' and the retention of every 'woman'.

2. A closely-allied rationale sometimes given is (as above) that the word *rōme* had two senses. But again, the proof is in the pudding. It's simply impossible to believe that

no instance of *rōme* in Thomas designated a male individual. There are, for example, five sayings which compare the kingdom to a person doing something-or-other. Two of these compare the kingdom to a woman; the other three compare it to a *rōme*. One would think that the originators intended some sort of balance between men and women in these sayings. But in Meyer-Patterson translations, that balance is lost. Instead, one gets two sayings comparing the kingdom to a woman, three comparing it to an ungendered 'person' (who, however, the pronouns clearly indicate to be a 'he').

3. A linguistic rationale that Meyer seemingly believes in is that the Coptic word *rōme* corresponds to Greek *anthrōpos*, which is said to be gender-neutral, as opposed to *anēr/andros*, which designates a male. The claimed correspondence simply isn't true, however. *Rōme* was used to translate *both anthrōpos* and *anēr/andros* in Coptic translations of the Greek NT. Evidently, then, the word *rōme* included *both* meanings in the minds of the Copts. Which did they intend in any given instance? We can only tell by looking at each instance individually, which is apparently what Layton and DeConick did. The Greek versions (P. Oxy. fragments) are of little help here, by the way, since only one saying parallel to a Coptic one containing *rōme* is extant.

Even if everything that rationale #3 assumes were true, however, it still doesn't follow that the word 'man' should disappear from English translations of Thomas. It hasn't, after all, disappeared from the Scholar's Version of the *canonical* gospels. Indeed, even in several places where there's a canonical passage that parallels a Thomas saying, and where the Greek has *anthrōpos*, the SV translation of the canonical passage has 'man' while Meyer-Patterson's Thomas parallel has 'person'.

There's a simple reason for that: the Greek experts on the SV translational panel didn't agree with Meyer and Patterson with respect to *anthrōpos*.

To my mind, the most crucial question is this: Is it at all likely that the originators of Coptic Thomas intended to refer to a generic woman from time to time, but *never* to a generic man? That, for example, they intended to compare the kingdom to a (generic) woman several times, but never to a (generic) man? In spite of their evident male-bias? Because I think that that isn't at all likely, I would downgrade the Meyer-Patterson family of translations, whatever their virtues, for their inaccuracy in this regard.

Mike Grondin, Aug, 2008

Jeremy Puma

Column: Perfect Day Living, Life as a Contemporary Gnostic

Right There Under Your Gnosis

We Gnostics love talking about just what this '*gnosis*' thing consists of, mainly because *if you have it, you can't describe it, nor will you typically admit it, and if you're trying to figure out what it is, you're likely wrong.* On occasion it's good to take what we think about gnosis out of our bag of tricks, toss it up against the wall and see if it still sticks. It's a tricky little devil, because it's different for everybody. Is it a secret? Is it enlightenment? Is it understanding? What is it? It's difficult to pin down in writing, because it's something that needs to be *experienced*. Although it's easy to get caught up in the whole myth cycle, Sophia, the Demiurge and all that crazy stuff, the religion isn't called 'Demiurgism' or 'Sophiolotry.' It's Gnosticism, so we'd better get some idea about just what we mean by this experience that's central to our religion.

Due to the many similarities between Buddhism and Gnosticism, gnosis is often equated with enlightenment of the 'whack-in-the-head' variety common to the Zen tradition. For very basic discussions, the two concepts probably are 'good enough for government work,' as it were. But, when we get into it, is the signified really one-to-one with the signifier? Is gnosis enlightenment in the 'flash of insight' sense? Really, isn't it kind of dishonest to both traditions to equate their experiences on an equivalent basis? *Let's divorce ourselves from the Buddhist idea of enlightenment for a moment and look at mentions of the experience from the Gnostic scriptures, and see what we can learn.* Unless otherwise noted, the selections that appear in this article are from *The Nag Hammadi Scriptures: International Edition*, edited by Marvin Meyer.

The *Second Revelation of James* describes gnosis as something someone is 'rich' in, and goes on to call its deliverer, the Christ, '*...one who alone was conceived from above.*' 'From above' indicates that gnosis is something that descends, like light from the Sun, then enriches someone. We often find, within Gnostic literature, that 'riches' symbolize living information or that inner part that processes it (*vide* 'The Hymn of the Pearl' or *The Gospel of Thomas*, Saying 63). So this author understood gnosis as **a** *singular comprehension* unlike any other, a new way of interfacing with reality, produced 'from above,' from the internal realms that correlate to the Pleromic levels of reality/cosmology. Gnosis, here, isn't something that happens to someone one time; rather, *it's an enhanced state of being or awareness.*

But, what happens to someone who achieves this state? Interestingly, evidence exists in the Gnostic corpus that *the experience of gnosis does not, in and of itself, grant one perfection.* Rather, it's the first step on a path which requires a reduction in 'sin' and leads to compassion for others. We find an example of this idea in the *Gospel of Philip* (emphasis mine):

> Whoever knows the truth is free, and a free person does not sin, for 'one who sins is a slave of sin....' Those who do not allow themselves to sin the world calls free. They do not allow themselves to sin, and the knowledge of the truth lifts them up—that is, it makes them free and superior to all. But 'love builds up.' *Whoever is free through knowledge is a slave because of love for those*

who do not yet have freedom of gnosis. Gnosis enables them to be free.

Since gnosis 'makes one free,' one is free to choose either compassion or egotism, either love or power. *Real gnosis, however, according to this Gospel, makes one into a servant, into a compassionate person who cares very deeply—is a slave—for other people.* The experience of gnosis doesn't make one into a 'holy person,' or into someone who is somehow 'beyond good and evil.' It doesn't give the right to look down on others with disdain. It gives one the choice to build relationships or tear them down; it extends one's awareness in such a capacity that one is more aware of the consequences of his or her actions, but is at a greater liberty to choose those consequences regardless.

Of course, the *internal* change granted by gnosis is the most radical. In the *Secret Book of James* we find the following admonition: 'Listen to the word, understand gnosis, love life, and no one will persecute you and no one will oppress you, other than you yourselves.' This passage implies an abiding inner peace in the person who has come to understand gnosis. Regardless of one's station in life, or the hardships one faces, gnosis illustrates that the reaction to these difficulties within one's life are one's complete responsibility. This is a far cry from the sentimentalist garbage spewed out by the 'You Create Your Own Reality' camp of 'The Secret' pushers. Note that gnosis does not automatically grant one the ability to love one's life; rather, gnosis compliments and enhances this ability. This is really a fairly radical idea; gnosis, as an experience, doesn't make one happy, but along with happiness it grants one a great deal of control over the way one perceives one's life. This also lends credence to the fact that, when experienced, *gnosis results in a heightened sense of awareness.* It increases one's ability to interface with one's surroundings.

The *Gospel of Truth* provides us with what is likely the best description of the post-gnosis responsibilities of the Gnostic, to which I refer as 'Perfect Day Living':

Speak from the heart, for you are the perfect day and in you dwells the light that does not fail. Speak of truth with those who seek it and of gnosis with those who have sinned in their error. Steady the feet of those who stumble and extend your hands to the sick. Feed the hungry and give rest to the weary. Awaken those who wish to arise and rouse those who sleep, for you embody vigorous understanding.

There is absolutely something spiritual and holy about gnosis. It would be silly to ignore how frequently it's referred to as 'awakening' or 'sobering up.' Meditation, prayer and sacrament are still the best and most often employed ways to achieve gnosis, and it is still a very distinctly religious phenomenon. Nonetheless, gnosis results in responsibility towards others. A far cry from the popular view of Gnosticism as a rebellion against the Demiurge or proto-feminist liberalism or psychedelic-fueled ecstasy, we find that gnosis really ends up having a lot to do with all of that kindness and compassion that Jesus kept going on about.

As we have seen, we can no longer honestly equate gnosis with Buddhist ideas of enlightenment. We have our own literature to draw from, and it is very explicit about what to expect from gnosis. The 'FLASH BANG' of enlightenment or epiphany can serve as a good metaphor, but it would be more accurate to think of this epiphany as the starter gun that begins the race. Gnosis allows for greater control over one's life, as well as greater satisfaction in whatever circumstances one finds one's self. It's more a slow, constant unfolding that needs continual vigilance to maintain than a small, infinitesimal peek at the Light. It's compassionate interaction with one's fellow beings, and love for other people. This is 'Perfect Day Living,' and will be the subject of this column.

Andrew Phillip Smith

Column: Into the Bridal Chamber

Romanticizing the Gnostics

I've just been watching a Youtube clip of Tim Freke speaking at a bookstore promotion in California. He was being challenged by a rather flamboyant looking Englishman who felt that Freke was romanticizing the Gnostics. The Englishman was probably right. Certainly, Freke and Gandy's reconstruction of early Christian history is selective, emphasising the deep spirituality of the Gnostics, whom Freke and Gandy see as being the original Christians, against what they see as the harsh dogma of literalist Christianity. In *The Jesus Mysteries* and *Jesus and the Lost Goddess*, the two writers draw on a generalised Gnostic teaching rather than on specific Gnostic texts to illustrate their own expression of a spirituality that, particularly in Freke's *Lucid Living*, has much in common with modern nondualism. It is a misty vision, projecting contemporary spiritual concerns into the past, and hence their historiography and exegesis could easily be seen as a romantic Gnosticism.

But what is wrong with being romantic? As Alan Moore says in the interview in this issue, 'I don't see what the hell is wrong with romanticism. It works. And it instils life with something that makes it worth living. It instils it with a spirit. It makes you feel that the world of ideas and spirit is a real and immediate one.'

Despite an insistent rationalism and scepticism, I must admit than I am, deep down, a romantic. Although I am sure that professional critics of literature, art and music might disagree with me, I see the essence of romanticism as the idealisation of a quality and the longing for that ideal in direct experience, failing which the ideal is injected into the world as a whole and

into the past in particular. Thus Wordsworth saw ideal Nature in the landscape of the English Lake District, while for many poets the personal beloved is seen as the living paradigm of Love itself.

Romanticism falls into danger when the longed-for quality is unworthy in itself. There is obviously something wrong with romanticizing the Nazis, and the romanticizing of violence itself is a difficult issue. Personally, I can be stirred by the revolt of the fourteenth-century Welshman Owain Glyndŵr, or by Irish rebel songs, and perhaps these tales of the oppressed are more worthy of a romantic approach than the glories of the empires of powerful nations. But this is still the romanticisation of violence. I remember listening uneasily to Shane MacGowan's song *Paddy Public Enemy Number One*, a paean to the IRA and INLA man Dominic McGlinchey who was responsible for many deaths before he himself was shot dead in a telephone box. But what is the difference between MacGowan's infamous song and, say, one of the beautiful and bloodthirsty Scottish border ballads? Perhaps nothing except the distance of time. Is MacGowan's eulogising of an IRA man really of a different quality to Homer's singing of the the brutality of Achilles, or indeed the extraordinary slaughters of the mythic Irish hero Cuchulainn?

It is also easy to romanticise the self-destructive creative person, the addict poet, acid-casualty rock star or junkie writer, especially if one has not seen the direct effect of abuse on an individual or on those close to him or her. Decadent romanticism hopes that the candle that is burnt at both ends will ignite into a brief blaze of final glory, rather than snuff itself out in a final culminatory fizzle.

The romanticizing of spirituality is somewhat different. Spirituality usually deals with some kind of distant aim or yearned-for superior state of being, and that is a right subject for romanticization. If one has a romantic tendency, it is certainly a good deal safer to romanticise something that lies in the distant past. Romanticizing a living spiritual teacher is dangerous because teachers are human and, as we all know in these times, subject to the most human tendencies of indulgence and corruption. So if one needs to romanticise, it is best to romanticise about some far off, hazily known epoch or group—the Knights Templar, the Cathars, the original disciples of Jesus, and the Gnostics. Of course, it's nice to ground your romanticism on the best available historical evidence, but the finest subjects for romance have an historical vagueness to them, a quality that is plentiful in all of the above groups.

The Gnostics are often upheld as worshippers of the divine feminine, largely through the influence of the *Da Vinci Code* and the sheaves of speculation on Mary Magdalen that preceded it and follow it. Despite the importance of Sophia in Gnostic myth, this notion has little foundation, and the pagan mystery cults, such as that devoted to Cybele, are better models for those who wish to revere the feminine. Yet what real harm is there in an inaccurate model of a goddess-based Gnosticism? The Gnostics are also held to be free thinkers, a concept that has much to do with the influence of Elaine Pagels' *The Gnostic Gospels*. They were almost certainly not such by our modern standards, but surely every generation has to remake the past in its own image.

Perhaps there are two forms of romanticism— the idealisation of a quality and then the longing for that quality in its most perfect form. Rosy romanticism has its flip side in unappeasable longing. I have certainly felt this myself at times, and in the late romantic English poets, such as Ernest Dowson or, in a different way, A. E. Houseman, the ideal romanticism of Shelley or Keats has become a yearning for the unattainable, and anything that can be actualised is no longer unattainable and therefore no longer the subject of longing. Certainly W.B. Yeats seemed no happier once he had sexual fulfilment, a wife and family and Ireland had independence. While living in London in the 1990s I remember experiencing a constant yearning for a mythologised version of my Welsh homeland only, on moving there for six months, to discover eventually a similar longing for London. Romantic longing is unappeasable, insatiable.

As Leonardo da Vinci wrote in his notebooks, 'Now you see that the hope and the desire of returning home and to one's former state is like the moth to the light, and that the man who with constant longing awaits with joy each new spring time, each new summer, each new month and new year— deeming that the things he longs for are ever too late in coming— does not perceive that he is longing for his own destruction. But this desire is the very quintessence, the spirit of the elements, which finding itself imprisoned with the soul is ever longing to return from the human body to its giver. And you must know that this same longing is that quintessence, inseparable from nature, and that man is the image of the world. '

Johann von Goethe moved from the subjective *Sturm-und-Drang* romanticism of his youth nto a maturity that valued the objective, which for him was the essence of classicism. The two approaches were seen as opposed to one another and he summed up his change of direction in the aphorism, 'the classical I call healthy and the romantic sick'.

A longing for wholeness, perfection, for the life of the spirit, for Gnosis is among the deepest of human needs. The dream of an ideal society of Gnostics may be legitimately projected back through history and may serve as an inspiration. This kind of romanticism becomes harmful only when it is a stumbling block to real experience. We cannot grant fulfilled Gnosis only to those who live in the distant past, and leave nothing for our present reality.

Mark Twain

Letters from Earth

Written by Mark Twain in 1909 and only published posthumously, *Letters from the Earth* consists of a set of missives from the archangel Satan to the archangels Michael and Raphael. Satan's observations comprise a satire on Christianity as Twain saw it in late nineteenth and early twentieth century United States. Twain is almost Marcionite in his contasting of the Old Testament and New Testament, but he isn't terribly impressed with either. His satirical intent and use of Satan as an exile is reminiscent of Gurdjieff's later *Beelzebub's Tales to His Grandson*. These two final letters contain Twain's most hilarious and pointed observations.

Letter X

The two Testaments are interesting, each in its own way. The Old one gives us a picture of these people's Deity as he was before he got religion, the other one gives us a picture of him as he appeared afterward. The Old Testament is interested mainly in blood and sensuality. The New one in Salvation. Salvation by fire.

The first time the Deity came down to earth, he brought life and death; when he came the second time, he brought hell.

Life was not a valuable gift, but death was. Life was a fever-dream made up of joys embittered by sorrows, pleasure poisoned by pain, a dream that was a nightmare-confusion of spasmodic and fleeting delights, ecstasies, exultations, happinesses, interspersed with long-drawn miseries, griefs, perils, horrors, disappointments, defeats, humiliations, and despairs—the heaviest curse devisable by divine ingenuity; but death was sweet, death was gentle, death was kind; death healed the bruised spirit and the broken heart, and gave them rest and forgetfulness; death was man's best friend; when man could endure life no longer, death came and set him free.

In time, the Deity perceived that death was a mistake; a mistake, in that it was insufficient; insufficient, for the reason that while it was an admirable agent for the inflicting of misery upon the survivor, it allowed the dead person himself to escape from all further persecution in the blessed refuge of the grave. This was not satisfactory. A way must be conceived to pursue the dead beyond the tomb.

The Deity pondered this matter during four thousand years unsuccessfully, but as soon as he came down to earth and became a Christian his mind cleared and he knew what to do. He invented hell, and proclaimed it.

Now here is a curious thing. It is believed by everybody that while he was in heaven he was stern, hard, resentful, jealous, and cruel; but that when he came down to earth and assumed the name Jesus Christ, he became the opposite of what he was before: that is to say, he became sweet, and gentle, merciful, forgiving, and all harshness disappeared from his nature and a deep and yearning love for his poor human children took its place. Whereas it was as Jesus Christ that he devised hell and proclaimed it!

Which is to say, that as the meek and gentle Savior he was a thousand billion times crueler than ever he was in the Old Testament—oh, incomparably more atrocious than ever he was when he was at the very worst in those old days!

Meek and gentle? By and by we will examine this popular sarcasm by the light of the hell which he invented.

While it is true that the palm for malignity must be granted to Jesus, the inventor of hell, he was hard and ungentle enough for all godlike purposes even before he became a Christian. It does not appear that he ever stopped to reflect that he was to blame when a man went wrong, inasmuch as the man was merely acting in accordance with the disposition he had afflicted him with. No, he punished the man, instead of punishing himself. Moreover, the punishment usually oversized the offense. Often, too, it fell, not upon the doer of a misdeed, but upon somebody else—a chief man, the head of a community, for instance.

And Israel abode in Shittim, and the people began to commit whoredom with the daughters of Moab.

And the Lord said unto Moses, Take all the heads of the people, and hang them up before the Lord against the Sun, that the fierce anger of the Lord may be turned away from Israel.

Does that look fair to you? It does not appear that the 'heads of the people' got any of the adultery, yet it is they that are hanged, instead of 'the people.'

If it was fair and right in that day it would be fair and right today, for the pulpit maintains that God's justice is eternal and unchangeable; also that he is the Fountain of Morals, and that his morals are eternal and unchangeable.

Very well, then, we must believe that if the people of New York should begin to commit whoredom with the daughters of New Jersey, it would be fair and right to set up a gallows in front of the city hall and hang the mayor and the sheriff and the judges and the archbishop on it, although they did not get any of it. It does not look right to me.

Moreover, you may be quite sure of one thing: it couldn't happen. These people would not allow it. They are better than their Bible. Nothing would happen here, except some lawsuits, for damages, if the incident couldn't be hushed up; and even down South they would not proceed against persons who did not get any of it; they would get a rope and hunt for the correspondents, and if they couldn't find them they would lynch a nigger.

Things have greatly improved since the Almighty's time, let the pulpit say what it may.

Will you examine the Deity's morals and disposition and conduct a little further? And will you remember that in the Sunday school the little children are urged to love the Almighty, and honor him, and praise him, and make him their model and try to be as like him as they can? Read:

1 And the Lord spake unto Moses, saying,

2 Avenge the children of Israel of the Midianites: afterward shalt thou be gathered unto thy people....

7 And they warred against the Midianites, as the Lord commanded Moses; and they slew all the males.

8 And they slew the kings of Midian, beside the rest of them that were slain; namely, Evi, and Rekem, and Zur, and Hur, and Reba, five kings of Midian: Balaam also the son of Beor they slew with the sword.

9 And the children of Israel took all the women of Midian captives, and their little ones, and took the spoil of all their cattle, and all their flocks, and all their goods.

10 And they burnt all their cities wherein they dwelt, and all their goodly castles, with fire.

11 And they took all the spoil, and all the prey, both of men and of beasts.

12 And they brought the captives, and the prey, and the spoil unto Moses, and Eleazar the priest, and unto the congregation of the children of Israel, unto the camp at the plains of Moab, which are by Jordan near Jericho.

13 And Moses, and Eleazar the priest, and all the princes of the congregation, went forth to meet them without the camp.

14 And Moses was wroth with the officers of the host, with the captains over thousands, and captains over hundreds, which came from the battle.

15 And Moses said unto them, Have ye saved all the women alive?

16 Behold, these caused the children of Israel, through the counsel of Balaam, to commit trespass against the Lord in the matter of Peor, and there was a plague among the congregation of the Lord.

17 Now therefore kill every male among the little ones, and kill every woman that hath known man by lying with him.

18 But all the women children, that have not known a man by lying with him, keep alive for yourselves.

19 And do ye abide without the camp seven days: whosoever hath killed any person, and whosoever hath touched any slain, purify both yourselves and your captives on the third day, and on the seventh day.

20 And purify all your raiment, and all that is made of skins, and all work of goats' hair, and all things made of wood.

21 And Eleazar the priest said unto the men of war which went to the battle, This is the ordinance of the law which the Lord commanded Moses....

25 And the Lord spake unto Moses, saying,

26 Take the sum of the prey that was taken, both of man and of beast, thou, and Eleazar the priest, and the chief fathers of the congregation:

27 And divide the prey into two parts; between them that took the war upon them, who went out to battle, and between all the congregation:

28 And levy a tribute unto the Lord of the men of war which went out to battle....

31 And Moses and Eleazar the priest did as the Lord commanded Moses.

32 And the booty, being the rest of the prey which the men of war had caught, was six hundred thousand and seventy thousand and five thousand sheep,

33 And threescore and twelve thousand beeves,

34 And threescore and one thousand asses,

35 And thirty and two thousand persons in all, of woman that had not known man by lying with him....

40 And the persons were sixteen thousand; of which the Lord's tribute was thirty and two persons.

41 And Moses gave the tribute, which was the Lord's heave offering, unto Eleazar the priest, as the Lord commanded Moses....

47 Even of the children of Israel's half, Moses took one portion of fifty, both of

man and of beast, and gave them unto the Levites, which kept the charge of the tabernacle of the Lord; as the Lord commanded Moses.

10 When thou comest nigh unto a city to fight against it, then proclaim peace unto it....

13 And when the Lord thy God hath delivered it into thine hands, thou shalt smite every male thereof with the edge of the sword:

14 But the women, and the little ones, and the cattle, and all that is in the city, even all the spoil thereof, shalt thou take unto thyself; and thou shalt eat the spoil of thine enemies, which the Lord thy God hath given thee.

15 Thus shalt thou do unto all the cities which are very far off from thee, which are not of the cities of these nations.

16 But of the cities of these people, which the Lord thy God doth give thee for an inheritance, thou shalt save alive nothing that breatheth:

The Biblical law says: 'Thou shalt not kill.'

The law of God, planted in the heart of man at his birth, says: 'Thou shalt kill.'

The chapter I have quoted shows you that the book-statute is once more a failure. It cannot set aside the more powerful law of nature.

According to the belief of these people, it was God himself who said: 'Thou shalt not kill.'

Then it is plain that he cannot keep his own commandments.

He killed all those people—every male.

They had offended the Deity in some way. We know what the offense was, without looking; that is to say, we know it was a trifle;

some small thing that no one but a god would attach any importance to. It is more than likely that a Midianite had been duplicating the conduct of one Onan, who was commanded to 'go into his brother's wife'—which he did; but instead of finishing, 'he spilled it on the ground.' The Lord slew Onan for that, for the lord could never abide indelicacy. The Lord slew Onan, and to this day the Christian world cannot understand why he stopped with Onan, instead of slaying all the inhabitants for three hundred miles around—they being innocent of offense, and therefore the very ones he would usually slay. For that had always been his idea of fair dealing. If he had had a motto, it would have read, 'Let no innocent person escape.' You remember what he did in the time of the flood. There were multitudes and multitudes of tiny little children, and he knew they had never done him any harm; but their relations had, and that was enough for him: he saw the waters rise toward their screaming lips, he saw the wild terror in their eyes, he saw that agony of appeal in the mothers' faces which would have touched any heart but his, but he was after the guiltless particularly, than he drowned those poor little chaps.

And you will remember that in the case of Adam's posterity all the billions are innocent—none of them had a share in his offense, but the Deity holds them guilty to this day. None gets off, except by acknowledging that guilt—no cheaper lie will answer.

Some Midianite must have repeated Onan's act, and brought that dire disaster upon his nation. If that was not the indelicacy that outraged the feelings of the Deity, then I know what it was: some Midianite had been pissing against the wall. I am sure of it, for that was an impropriety which the Source of all Etiquette never could stand. A person could piss against a tree, he could piss on his mother, he could piss on his own breeches, and get off, but he must not piss against the wall—that would be going quite too far. The origin of the divine prejudice against this humble crime is not stated; but we know that the prejudice was very strong—so strong that nothing but a wholesale massacre of the people inhabiting the region where the wall was defiled could satisfy the Deity.

Take the case of Jeroboam. 'I will cut off from Jeroboam him that pisseth against the wall.' It was done. And not only was the man that did it cut off, but everybody else.

The same with the house of Baasha: everybody was exterminated, kinsfolks, friends, and all, leaving 'not one that pisseth against a wall.'

In the case of Jeroboam you have a striking instance of the Deity's custom of not limiting his punishments to the guilty; the innocent are included. Even the 'remnant' of that unhappy house was removed, even 'as a man taketh away dung, till it be all gone.' That includes the women, the young maids, and the little girls. All innocent, for they couldn't piss against a wall. Nobody of that sex can. None but members of the other sex can achieve that feat.

A curious prejudice. And it still exists. Protestant parents still keep the Bible handy in the house, so that the children can study it, and one of the first things the little boys and girls learn is to be righteous and holy and not piss against the wall. They study those passages more than they study any others, except those which incite to masturbation. Those they hunt out and study in private. No Protestant child exists who does not masturbate. That art is the earliest accomplishment his religion confers upon him. Also the earliest her religion confers upon her.

The Bible has this advantage over all other books that teach refinement and good

manners: that it goes to the child. It goes to the mind at its most impressible and receptive age—the others have to wait.

'Thou shalt have a paddle upon thy weapon; and it shall be, when thou wilt ease thyself abroad, thou shalt dig therewith, and shalt turn back and cover that which cometh from thee.'

That rule was made in the old days because 'The Lord thy God walketh in the midst of thy camp.'

It is probably not worthwhile to try to find out, for certain, why the Midianites were exterminated. We can only be sure that it was for no large offense; for the cases of Adam, and the Flood, and the defilers of the wall teach us that much. A Midianite may have left his paddle at home and thus brought on the trouble. However, it is no matter. The main thing is the trouble itself, and the morals of one kind and another that it offers for the instruction and elevation of the Christian of today.

God wrote upon the tables of stone: 'Thou shalt not kill.' Also: 'Thou shalt not commit adultery.'

Paul, speaking by the divine voice, advised against sexual intercourse altogether. A great change from the divine view as it existed at the time of the Midianite incident.

Letter XI

Human history in all ages is red with blood, and bitter with hate, and stained with cruelties; but not since Biblical times have these features been without a limit of some kind. Even the Church, which is credited with having spilt more innocent blood, since the beginning of its supremacy, than all the political wars put together have spilt, has observed a limit. A sort of limit. But you notice that when the

Lord God of Heaven and Earth, adored Father of Man, goes to war, there is no limit. He is totally without mercy—he, who is called the Fountain of Mercy. He slays, slays, slays! All the men, all the beasts, all the boys, all the babies; also all the women and all the girls, except those that have not been deflowered.

He makes no distinction between innocent and guilty. The babies were innocent, the beasts were innocent, many of the men, many of the women, many of the boys, many of the girls were innocent, yet they had to suffer with the guilty. What the insane Father required was blood and misery; he was indifferent as to who furnished it.

The heaviest punishment of all was meted out to persons who could not by any possibility have deserved so horrible a fate—the 32,000 virgins. Their naked privacies were probed, to make sure that they still possessed the hymen unruptured; after this humiliation they were sent away from the land that had been their home, to be sold into slavery; the worst of slaveries and the shamefulest, the slavery of prostitution; bed-slavery, to excite lust, and satisfy it with their bodies; slavery to any buyer, be he gentleman or be he a coarse and filthy ruffian.

It was the Father that inflicted this ferocious and undeserved punishment upon those bereaved and friendless virgins, whose parents and kindred he had slaughtered before their eyes. And were they praying to him for pity and rescue, meantime? Without a doubt of it.

These virgins were 'spoil' plunder, booty. He claimed his share and got it. What use had he for virgins? Examine his later history and you will know.

His priests got a share of the virgins, too. What use could priests make of virgins? The private history of the Roman Catholic confessional can answer that question for you.

The confessional's chief amusement has been seduction—in all the ages of the Church. Père Hyacinth testifies that of a hundred priests confessed by him, ninety-nine had used the confessional effectively for the seduction of married women and young girls. One priest confessed that of nine hundred girls and women whom he had served as father and confessor in his time, none had escaped his lecherous embrace but he elderly and the homely. The official list of questions which the priest is required to ask will overmasteringly excite any woman who is not a paralytic.

There is nothing in either savage or civilized history that is more utterly complete, more remorselessly sweeping than the Father of Mercy's campaign among the Midianites. The official report does not furnish the incidents, episodes, and minor details, it deals only in information in masses: all the virgins, all the men, all the babies, all 'creatures that breathe,' all houses, all cities; it gives you just one vast picture, spread abroad here and there and yonder, as far as eye can reach, of charred ruin and storm-swept desolation; your imagination adds a brooding stillness, an awful hush—the hush of death. But of course there were incidents. Where shall we get them?

Out of history of yesterday's date. Out of history made by the red Indian of America. He has duplicated God's work, and done it in the very spirit of God. In 1862 the Indians in Minnesota, having been deeply wronged and treacherously treated by the government of the United States, rose against the white settlers and massacred them; massacred all they could lay their hands upon, sparing neither age nor sex. Consider this incident:

Twelve Indians broke into a farmhouse at daybreak and captured the family. It consisted of the farmer and his wife and four daughters, the youngest aged fourteen and the eldest eighteen. They crucified the parents; that is to say, they stood them stark naked against the wall of the living room and nailed their hands to the wall. Then they stripped the daughters bare, stretched them upon the floor in front of their parents, and repeatedly ravished them. Finally they crucified the girls against the wall opposite this parents, and cut off their noses and their breasts. They also—but I will not go into that. There is a limit. There are indignities so atrocious that the pen cannot write them. One member of that poor crucified family—the father—was still alive when help came two days later.

Now you have one incident of the Minnesota massacre. I could give you fifty. They would cover all the different kinds of cruelty the brutal human talent has ever invented.

And now you know, by these sure indications, what happened under the personal direction of the Father of Mercies in his Midianite campaign. The Minnesota campaign was merely a duplicate of the Midianite raid. Nothing happened in the one that didn't happen in the other.

No, that is not strictly true. The Indian was more merciful than was the Father of Mercies. He sold no virgins into slavery to minister to the lusts of the murderers of their kindred while their sad lives might last; he raped them, then charitably made their subsequent sufferings brief, ending them with the precious gift of death. He burned some of the houses, but not all of them. He carried out innocent dumb brutes, but he took the lives of none.

Would you expect this same conscienceless God, this moral bankrupt, to become a teacher of morals; of gentleness; of meekness; of righteousness; of purity? It looks impossible, extravagant; but listen to him. These are his own words: Blessed are the poor in spirit, for theirs is the kingdom of heaven.

Blessed are they that mourn, for they shall

be comforted.

Blessed are the meek, for they shall inherit the earth.

Blessed are they which do hunger and thirst after righteousness, for they shall be filled.

Blessed are the merciful, for they shall obtain mercy.

Blessed are the pure in heart, for they shall see God.

Blessed are the peacemakers, for they shall be called the children of God.

Blessed are they which are persecuted for righteousness' sake, for theirs is the kingdom of heaven.

Blessed are ye, when men shall revile you, and persecute you, and say all manner of evil against you falsely, for my sake.

The mouth that uttered these immense sarcasms, these giant hypocrisies, is the very same that ordered the wholesale massacre of the Midianitish men and babies and cattle; the wholesale destruction of house and city; the wholesale banishment of the virgins into a filthy and unspeakable slavery. This is the same person who brought upon the Midianites the fiendish cruelties which were repeated by the red Indians, detail by detail, in Minnesota eighteen centuries later. The Midianite episode filled him with joy. So did the Minnesota one, or he would have prevented it.

The Beatitudes and the quoted chapters from Numbers and Deuteronomy ought always to be read from the pulpit together; then the congregation would get an all-round view of Our Father in Heaven. Yet not in a single instance have I ever known a clergyman to do this.

Water and Fire by Scott Finch

Book Reviews

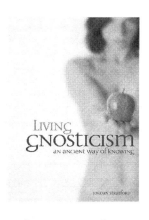

Living Gnosticism, Jordan Stratford, Apocryphile Press, 132pp, £7.95/$14.95

Living Gnosticism by Jordan Stratford (a priest of the Apostolic Johannite Church) is intended as an introductory text to the Gnostic tradition, providing not only the historical and academic background that is rife within the selection of books currently available on the subject, but also (and more primarily) the living, breathing, practical tradition of modern Gnostics embracing God, Christ, Sophia, etc., on a daily basis.

The first thing that struck me about this book is its slimness. Of course, the majority of texts dealing with Gnosticism are academic in focus, so it's easy to see where the difference in size comes from. When Stratford announced the book in the first place, however, I must admit that I was expecting something quite different (more a manual than an introductory text, which he aimed towards with his first book, The DaVinci Prayerbook). Indeed, Stratford invited the online Gnostic community (through his blog, Ecclesia Gnostica in Nova Albion) to contribute to the book by emailing him their thoughts and opinion on what Gnosticism is, what it means to them, and how they approach it as a contemporary religion. All of this is missing from the book, perhaps replaced by quotations from various scriptures, songs, and poems, lending it to be a book entirely different to my expectations.

But is that a good thing? In some ways, yes, as Straford's wit, humour, and undeniable eloquence delivers strongly in the passages he writes. The first half of the book deals with the main topics and themes of Gnosticism (Gnosis, the Demiurge, Sophia, etc.), while the last two quarters deal with the liturgical year (predominantly featuring suitable extracts from gospels and other texts) and a Questions & Answers section respectively. Stratford had originally included a glossary and chronology, which would have bumped it up another fifty or so pages, but he decided in the end that such sections wouldn't be of much interest to his target audience (perhaps confounding more than illuminating). In a sense then it's easy to see why the book is so slim – though I would have to question the inclusion of the liturgical year section here, as I'm not sure a casual reader looking for an introduction to Gnosticism will find this section very appealing.

If you're already familiar with Gnosticism (even if only through Stratford's blog), then you won't really learn anything new here. Indeed, Stratford's own words sum up the target audience quite nicely: 'I didn't write this book for Gnostics so much as I wrote it for Gnostics' moms'. Does that mean the book is of no value to fully-fledged practicing Gnostics? Not really. The sheer library of beautiful quotations Stratford has amassed and included in this slim book is worth the price alone, as are, indeed, his own poetic musings. Just don't expect much in the way of information or historical backing.

Speaking of historical backing, it's hard not to notice that Stratford has a tendency to make sweeping statements about Gnosticism, such as its origin: 'Gnosticism is a pre-Christian religious tradition [...] Originating in the intellectual 'café societies' of Alexandria around 200 BCE.' Apart from the acquired taste analogies he uses (there's only so far you can equate Alexandria to Starbucks before the analogy wears thin), there is absolutely no historical backing for such a statement. As a practicing Gnostic, my own personal conviction is that Gnosticism did indeed exist in some form around this period, perhaps with a strong oral tradition, but I simply have no evidence to back up that claim, so it will remain a personal opinion. I would have no quarrel if Stratford made it obvious that he was merely stating his opinion here, but a casual reader who is not already familiar with Gnosticism (such as the target audience) will undoubtedly come away from reading the book thinking that Stratford's opinion is historical fact.

The same issue comes to the fore with his insistence that the ecclesiastical and liturgical trappings of the ancient and modern churches are part and parcel of the entire Gnostic movement, which simply isn't the case. Indeed, at several points he states that Gnostics look like Catholics but are Buddhists on the inside (a very poignant idea, which has a lot of truth when it comes to the ecclesiastical Gnostics), but this assumes that all Gnostics have an affinity for the ecclesiastical. As a priest himself, it can be perhaps forgiven that he would be so biased, but I believe that this book could have benefited from more honesty on the fact that what he's portraying is merely one form of Gnosticism – admittedly the primary form as it is in the modern world, with the various Gnostic churches supporting this, and one that I am personally an adherent of. Again, a casual reader who knows nothing of Gnosticism before reading this book will walk away thinking all Gnostics embrace the Valentinian form.

A final example is the extremely broad categorization of Gnosticism that Stratford uses, including many sects and groups that are perhaps better classed as sister traditions than as part of the Great Mother Gnosticism herself. He frequently cites Hermeticism and Paganism, among other traditions, and tends to highlight all of the great thinkers and artists of the world as Gnostics, which comes off a little like propaganda to sell Gnosticism to the modern world, or perhaps it could be classed as an apologetic piece, starting off immediately defending Gnosticism from all the 'bad press' it has admittedly received over the centuries.

One might criticize the book for the fact that at least half of it is made up of quotations, and what isn't quoted tends to lack historical backing, but it's hard to deny that Stratford knows what Gnosticism is *today*, as a modern, living, growing tradition, illuminating the lives of many as they embrace its teachings in scripture old and new, in the art and poetry of its famous supporters, and in the everyday hustle and bustle of contemporary life.

Dean Wilson

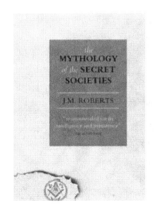

The Mythology of the Secret Societies, J. M. Roberts, Watkins Publishing, 480pp, £12.99/$19.95.

Professor J. M. Roberts, who died in 2003, has been justifiably described as one of the leading historical minds of his generation. With titles such as *The History of the World* and *The Twentieth Century* to his name, we can see that Roberts had the rare gift of grasping and communicating the broader view, taking in (as his obituarist put it) 'the full sweep of the past', while scrupulously avoiding the pitfalls of dogma and over-schematisation. This perspective, it might be noted, has enabled him to offer refreshingly level-headed views on a range of subjects from global warming to the significance of 9/11. Here, in *The Mythology of the Secret Societies* (first publish in 1973) we find Roberts on his scholarly 'home-turf', discussing an area of historical enquiry where he first cut his academic teeth.

The book offers an academic study what we would nowadays refer to as 'the Conspiracy Theory' – the view that all significant historical events are masterminded by a secretive yet omnipotent cabal, pulling strings behind a succession of wars, revolutions and economic crises. Variants of this myth have of course existed, and continue to exist, in many different forms all over the world: with the conspiractors variously identified as the Jews, the Knights Templars, nocturnal witches, the Bilderberg group, COMINTERN, the CIA or even the British Royal family. But Roberts concentrates here on a specific manifestation of this fertile aspect of the human social imagination, centring on the rumours and suspicions surrounding the Freemasons and related confraternities in eighteenth and nineteenth century Europe.

Roberts wastes little time pondering on the positive value these claims in themselves. The notion of an organised plot orchestrated by secret societies is unequivocally dismissed, as are the lurid speculation surrounding the goings on behind the doors of the Masonic lodge. What interests Roberts is not so much the veracity of this material, as *why* our predecessors were so ready to believe in 'this farrago of nonsense' – which he identifies as primarily the product of political paranoia of the post-Revolutionary age.

Such a blunt vindication would be not be satisfactory without at least some attempt to disclose the reality of the secret societies themselves, and their actual relationship (whether real or imagined) with the wider political culture of the day. Fortunately, Roberts offers a well-researched and balanced evaluation of the available evidence, although as he admits

that reliable documentation pertaining to the secret societies is, by its very nature, both hard to come by and problematic in terms of its evaluation. As he puts it in the Preface 'there is no clear line between the mythological and positive history of secret societies'. For this reason, Roberts sensible avoids prolonged speculation about the more remote origins of the Freemasons, or the Italo-French Carbonarii – both of which, it would appear, seem to have emerged innocuously enough out of the late-Medieval guild system. The merest whiff of the Holy Blood and the Holy Grail is offered by a brief discussion of the supposed connection with the persecuted order of the Knights Templar – a pedigree which is firmly (and no doubt accurately) relegated to the realms of spurious mythology. Beyond this, almost nothing is said of the ritual practices (real or imagined), belief systems or spiritual ideology of Freemasonry or the other confraternities. This is first and foremost a study of the political, rather than philosophical or esoteric aspects of the secret society.

Such academic self-restraint may disappoint some readers, and there are times when one feels Roberts goes a little too far in his quietist assessment of the thought-world of the Masonic lodge. At one stage he quotes, evidently with some approval, one pro-Masonic pamphleteer, who pointed out that the health of the king was regularly toasted, and that 'there was no talk of either religion or politics, not even of scandal' at Masonic social occasions. One can't help wondering how conversations were filled at the lodge dinners if all of these topics remained resolutely off the agenda. The reality appears to have been – as the evidence presented in this book does not quite succeed in refuting – that confraternities of this kind were in fact little different from any other places where men met and talked in the eighteenth and nineteenth centuries: coffee houses, university societies, drinking clubs or religious congregations. Given the fraught atmosphere of the post-revolutionary Europe, it would be more than a little surprising if the political or religious issues of the day were not given an occasional airing in the confidential and sophisticated environment of the society lodge.

The pivotal event of this period was the French Revolution and, as Roberts makes clear, the specific charge of political conspiracy attributed to the Freemasons and other secret societies gained a peculiar potency in the aftermath of this singular cataclysmic event. One particularly colourful myth, which gained widespread currency in nineteenth century Europe, saw the French Revolution as an act of retribution orchestrated by the Freemasons, in fulfilment of an ancient oath of revenge against the House of Bourbon for their oppression of the Knights Templar in the time of Philip V. Nonsense, of course, but as Roberts points out, some of the more romantic-minded Freemasons themselves had not been entirely innocent of adding fuel to the fire, with their own colourful claims of ancient origins and chivalric connections. A fashion for the exotic 'Scottish rite' masonry prevailed in Paris during the middle decades of the eighteenth century, and it was during this time that the occult and mystical elements of the Masonic myth became crystallised – often perpetuated by those claiming to be masons themselves. The proliferation of non-orthodox or pseudo-masonic organisations around this time, Roberts concludes, makes any general pronouncement about masonry in general unreliable if not demonstrably false. This did not prevent, however, the wilder excesses of some of these fringe organisations from tarring the reputation of masonry as a whole, and contributing a few grains of truth to burgeoning mythology of the secret society.

A case in point is the phenomenon of the Illuminati, an organisation that some readers will be surprised to learn did have an existence outside the realms of comic-book parody. Founded in 1776 in the conservative heartlands of Catholic Bavaria, the Illuminati has always been accorded a special place within the demonology of the secret society mythos. This was at least partly down its own grandiose projections; its strategy of infiltrating and assuming control of mainstream Masonic lodges; its system of elite higher grades, affording initiation into the covert agenda of the organisation; and, most significant of all, its political and revolutionary intimations.

As Roberts makes clear, the reality behind the myth of the Illuminati was considerably more mundane than either its supporters or its numerous and powerful enemies appear to have believed at the time. Its origin may be traced back to an undergraduate society, whose interests in the literature of the enlightenment probably would have been considered harmless anywhere outside the church-dominated university culture from which it initially emerged. For all its talk of revolution, the aim of its founder Adam Weishaupt appears to have involved little more than a modest programme of liberal reform by means of peaceful infiltration of local and national government offices by its senior members. Yet, within the context of the pre-revolutionary period, such aspirations could easily assume a more sinister complexion. Magnified by the lens of institutional paranoia, wilfully obscured by its own a culture of self-mystification, the Illuminati were to assume a stature and significance out of all proportion, giving a tangible form to the whelter of suspicion growing up around the notion of the secret society in Europe at the time. Following a pattern that echoed in many respects the witch-craze of two centuries earlier, confirmation of the power and extent of the Illuminati were quickly extracted from witnesses arrested in the 'Illuminati panic' of the late 1780s: some of whom may have been subject to torture or other coercive means, others of whom were only to willing to ingratiate themselves with authorities by telling them what it was they plainly wanted to hear. The case of the Illuminati illustrates with almost comic clarity the looking-glass *folie a deux* out of which this delusive mythology was born.

The shocking excesses of the French Revolution, and the terror it inspired in the ruling classes of Europe, were the decisive factor in locking the mythology of the secret society into the mainstream of political throughout the nineteenth century. As Roberts points out early on in this book, the belief in and fear of secret societies was most characteristic of the conservative position. Men from the clerical orders, or the aristocratic magnates of the *ancien regime*, may well have looked in horror and disbelief at the liberal reforms enacted by governments in the post-revolutionary epoch, and found in the myth of the secret society a plausible explanation for these bewildering changes. As Roberts affirms, his study has this very specific focus, being 'all about the delusions of the directing class – we are not dealing with a mass phenomenon such as popular anti-semitism'.

This restriction of focus is both admirable and, it must be, at times rather frustrating. Roberts devotes much of the middle of the book to a comprehensive trawl through the legal and administrative archives of France and Italy in the Napoleonic and Reformation eras, discussing the police theories of secret society organisation, and its involvement with the broader politics of the Muratist or Sanfedisti movements, for example. Here, one suspects, Roberts' specialist interest in the Italian republic 1802-1805 may have played a part in determining the focus of what, even in its restricted definition, is really a far broader subject.

Roberts identifies the period between 1815 and 1914 as the heyday of the myth of secret societies, yet (aside from a few revealing quotes and anecdotes in the opening chapter) has very little to say about the later part of this period (his analysis tends to focus on the early part of the Restoration era, i.e. the 1820s). He also has very little to say about the relationship of this mythology to more contemporary variants – not least the anti-semitism of the late nineteenth and twentieth centuries. The mythology of the secret society, as we know, did not come to an end in the 1830s or even in 1914 but still alive today – even if most of its adherents belong to what might be termed 'the tin-foil hat brigade'.

It would have been interesting to hear slightly more about the relationship between conspiracy theories associated with the Bilderberg group, the Zionist lobby or the Bohemian grove circle in America and the mythology of the secret societies perpetuated in Europe of the eighteenth and nineteenth centuries – and perhaps also some explanation of the key differences. Why, for example, it was that the Conspiracy Theory was a 'delusion of the directing class' in the eighteenth and nineteenth centuries, yet seems to be most characteristic of marginal and disempowered groups in the twentieth and twenty-first centuries? Roberts makes a few tentative steps towards some general conclusions on the structure and dynamics of the conspiracy mythology, but stops short of what anything that feels like a satisfactory general conclusion. Perhaps this would be too much to ask in a rigourous academic study of this kind. A more popular work, such as Jon Ronson's *Them: Adventures with Extremists*, might be the place to look for an accessible, light-hearted and easy-to-swallow general theory of the conspiracy myth with a more contemporary emphasis. Instead, *The Mythology of the Secret Societies* offers a high-definition view into a fascinating period of European history, textured by a wealth of intriguing anecdotes and colourful personalities. If Roberts resists the temptation to project his own personality and belief system onto the material involved, the end result is an objective account of an extraordinary body of human expression and behaviour – which remains none the less intriguing as a result of remaining partially unexplained.

Will Parker

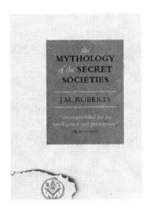

The Meditations of Marcus Aurelius: Annotated & Explained, Russell McNeil Sohaib N. Sultan, with a foreword by Jane I. Smith Skylight Paths 288pp £11.99/$16.99

The Qur'an and Sayings of the Prophet Muhammad: Annotated & Explained Skylight Paths, 204pp £11.99/$16.99

The Zohar: Annotated & Explained Skylight Paths; Daniel C. Matt with a foreword by Andrew Harvey, *135pp £10.99/ $15.99*

Skylight Paths' Annotated & Explained series covers a wide range of spiritual texts. Typically there is an introduction and other supporting material, a translation of the text and a commentary. The annotations are on the left hand page, the translation on the right. Somehow I always expect these to be the other way round, and I also find the design of these books, with their large san-serif typefaces rather unappealing. But the format lends itself well to elucidating the obscurities of the accompanying text, and the series has been consistently useful. The annotations typically explain obscure references, make brief comments on the historical or linguistic context of a passage, generally with a spirit of interreligious and intercultural cooperation and reciprocal respect.

The Meditations of Marcus Aurelius: Annotated & Explained Russell McNeil revising George Long's classic translation.

Marcus Aurelius' stark realisations are so incisive, his advice so assured, and his pantheism that verges on a nontheism so modern, that it is easy to forget that it all stands on a foundational structure of Stoic philosophy. On almost every page, McNeil reminds us of this philosophical structure, and indicates Aurelius' specific intentions and shows how this is more than a collection of insights and fatherly advice. McNeil's states that his intention is to show the reader 'how to reason like a Stoic', and I dare say that he has succeeded. Sometimes Long's Marcus Aurelius can give one goosebumps: 'And, to say all in a word, everything which belongs to the body is a stream, and what belongs to the soul is a dream and vapour, and life is a warfare and a stranger's sojourn, and after fame is oblivion.'

Sohaib N. Sultan, with a foreword by Jane I. Smith *The Qur'an and Sayings of the Prophet Muhammad: Annotated & Explained*

Once again, the series format allows the author to cherry pick interesting and relevant passages from the Qur'an and the hadith. Without this selection and commentary, the Qur'an can seem overwhelming. Sultan, also author of *The Koran For Dummies*, explains the Qur'an to non-Muslims. I must say that the approach is a little orthodox for my taste, emphasising the external side of Islam, the praxis rather than the Gnosis, but it communicates a good deal of the Muslim viewpoint, and I for one understand the principles of Islam better for reading this.

Daniel C. Matt with a foreword by Andrew Harvey *The Zohar: Annotated & Explained*

The introduction is brief, and the text is very lightly annotated, but the selections from this very difficult work are well chosen, and this would be an excellent first book for study of the Zohar, or even as an introduction to the Jewish Kabbbalah. Harvey's foreword is typically sentimental, and one hopes that his kabbalist friend named Ezekiel is not an invention.

Despite a few reservations about the format, all three of these books are excellent introductions to their respective texts.

Arthur Craddock

**The Way of Thomas, John R. Mabry, O Books
196pp £10.99/$19.95**

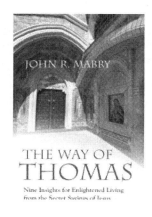

The Way of Thomas by John R. Mabry deals with a Gnostic/proto-Gnostic text that has seen a lot of attention in the last few decades: the Gospel of Thomas. It contains a new translation by Mabry, who compared various other translations and the Oxyrhynchus fragments, an interesting and informative introduction, and nine chapters dealing with what the author considers to be the key insights to understanding this mystical text.

First off we must deal with Mabry's translation. I read it through a few times and compared it to the main translations: Lambdin, Meyer, and Robinson (the latter two working with Patterson). However, I didn't find much new here. Indeed, most 'new' translations I've seen in recent years don't have very much 'new' about them, but what can we expect from something as short as the Gospel of Thomas and something that has been translated so many times? As far as I understand it, I would warrant that the author wanted to write about his nine insights, but also wanted to include a copy of the Gospel. Due to the limitations of 'fair use' in copyright (while the original text is no longer under copyright, the translation is) he is forced to come up with his own translation. He utilised Grondin's interlinear Coptic translation to aid his work, which may have helped him come to what he deems a more accurate translation – at the price of poetry, however, as the translation destroys the beautiful structure of the *logoi* that some of the more authoritative translations retain. He also modernises terminology which tends to weaken their impact. I personally prefer the Lambdin translation; while it may not be the most accurate, it is, I believe, much closer to the heart of the messages contained therein.

Once the reader delves into Mabry's thorough introduction it is clear that the author knows his stuff. An intriguing history is given, dealing with Jewish Christians, the apostles, Gnostics, Christ himself, and, of course, our very own Thomas the Twin and his school of thought and followers. For anyone unfamiliar with this history, Mabry gives a clear overview that doesn't get bogged down in academics, which many other texts tend to do. Ultimately this is a book geared at people looking for *insight*, as the sub-title reveals, so the target audience is only really looking for the basics when it comes to the historical side of things. What matters more are the nine chapters that follow.

This is where Mabry really shines. His insights have been expounded upon by many people over the years, but the clarity with which he deals with them is refreshing. This is a book that a practicing Gnostic of twenty years or a asual reader who only heard about this strange gospel yesterday can learn from. There is depth and simplicity all rolled into one, and Mabry deals with key teachings like unitive consciousness, the balance of religion and spirituality, and the fact that at the end of the day we are our own spiritual authorities. Even a casual read of this book shows that Mabry truly knows his stuff. As an added measure, he even throws in a few exercises to try at the end of each chapter, inviting the reader to *do* something as opposed to merely reading about it.

One of the few areas that I found fault with Mabry's treatment of the verses is his 'explaining away' of controversial substance – particularly that of *logion 114*, which contradicts the earlier 'make the two into one' comments we find in *logion 22* by saying that Jesus will make Mary 'male' so that she might enter the Kingdom of Heaven. This is understandably a provocative verse, and many claims of sexism are levelled at the text for this single saying, but Mabry's explanation is, I feel, somewhat lacking. He states that he believes there was an addendum to this verse, saying '…And any man who makes himself female, will likewise enter the Kingdom.' While I understand that the author feels the need to make the verse congruent with the earlier one, the theory that a celibate male scribe didn't like it so decided to leave out the last line in his transcription sounds like such a cop-out to me. Why this same scribe would retain the entirety of logion 22 and omit part of logion 114 that he didn't like doesn't make sense, but the fact of the matter is that we're confusing sex and gender here. Jesus is obviously not speaking about making Mary physically male (after all, transexuality would have been frowned upon even more in those days), and this is further emphasised by the use of 'Kingdom of Heaven', which Jesus makes clear to us is a spiritual reality, not a physical one, in many of the other verses. When we understand that most mythologies attribute the female gender to the earth (Earth Goddess, etc.) and the male to Heaven (Sky God, etc.), the idea of making female into male actually turns out to be the alchemical process of turning physical into spiritual (which is what this Gospel is all about). To note the allegory and symbolism of the other 113 verses and fail to see it in the 114th as well tends to reveal that those who have eyes to see don't really use them.

The Gospel of Thomas is a text that I have read and loved for years, and I have written about my own insights and interpretations of the verses in various places. However, this prior experience did not make reading *The Way of Thomas* a tedious task, as I thought it might be at first, having seen so many similar books on the topic. The insights are well-founded, and while I don't necessarily agree with them all, I found reading them to be a pleasure and extremely informative. The only real issue I have with the book is a few minor errors here and there, such as spelling the Tetragrammaton as YWHW instead of YHWH (which is a big mistake when we consider the Hebrew), and, of course, the treatment of the more controversial verses in the Gospel, as I outlined above.

The Way of Thomas joins many other books in

offering new translations and new insights into one of the most accessible (and paradoxically inaccessible) gospels we have in our possession. While even the author himself stated that it is best to come to your own understanding of the verses, for those who want to know what an elusive passage actually means or to add to their own understanding, you can't go wrong with this book.

Dean Wilson

The Golden Thread Joscelyn Godwin, Quest Publications, pp.£12.99/$16.95
Hidden Wisdom Richard Smoley and Jay Kinney Quest Publishing £16.99/$18.95

The Return of the Perennial Philosophy. John G. Holman. Watkins Publishing, 192pp. £10.99/$17.95

Western esotericism is a loosely defined tradition that includes Gnosticism, neoplatonism, alchemy, Hermetism and Hermeticism and magic. Until the Renaissance rediscovery of the Corpus Hermeticum united these various disciplines (excepting Gnosticism, for which interest was lacking, based partly on the lack of sources, until the nineteenth century) there was no unity to this tradition. A medieval alchemist would not have perceived himself as a magician, and neoplatonists, exemplified by Plotinus and Porphyry, were hostile to Gnostics and denied any equivalence between their philosophy and Gnosticism. Yet Renaissance Hermeticism and nineteenth-century occultism have passed on to us a somewhat unified tradition, and now western esotericism may be considered as a tree with many branches.

These three recent, or recently reissued books do a good job of introducing the reader to the tradition and suggest lines of further study and practice.

The Golden Thread is a slim volume (aside from its interesting footnotes and a foreword by Richard Smoley, it occupies a mere 152 pages) written by Jocelyn Godwin, who is both an expert in the esoteric tradition and a scholar of music. Godwin manages to cover the Chaldean Oracles, Platonism, Pythagoreanism, Orphism, Hermetism, Gnosticism, the Gothic cathedrals, Sufism, negative theology, modern traditions and much more. The tone of these essays is light, but the scholarship behind them is by no means lightweight and Godwin displays an enviable ability to cut to the chase and each chapter contains sharp insights. It can be recommended as a first introduction to the tradition, but also contains a good deal for anyone who wishes to refresh their knowledge or to have a taste of Godwin's approach.

Richard Smoley and Jay Kinney's *Hidden Wisdom* covers similar ground at greater length, with a broader selection of traditions. This revised edition draws on the pair's extensive experience as editors of the excellent but now defunct *Gnosis* magazine. Chapters on Gnosticism, esoteric Christianity, Kabbalah, Freemasonry, alchemy, magic, Shamanism, the Gurdjieff tradition, etc., lay out the fundamentals of each approach, with astute suggestions for further reading at the end of each section. There isn't too much in the way of synthesis, but this means that each tradition is presented accurately, in its own terms. Godwin's approach relies more on distillation, and has more in the way of value judgment, while this is more of a standard introduction—but no less valuable for that.

John Holman's *The Return of the Perennial Philosophy* is less of a general survey than an attempt at synthesising a new direction for western esotericism. (The term 'perennial philosophy' was coined in the sixteenth century, but made famous by the philosopher Leibnitz,

and more recently revived by Aldous Huxley in his book of the same name.) Holman begins with the premise that even academic study of the perennial philosophy must acknowledge that the tradition is based on inner experience and cannot be usefully examined without this— western esotericism is not a set of intellectual systems or a variety of external praxes. Holman is very eclectic, but somehow manages to create a convincing system which finds common ground in many traditions and creates a structure which clarifies the commonality of these traditions without misrepresenting them. He identifies a very Gurdjieffian preponderance of references to three (usually representing a divine triad or trinity) and seven (usually associated with an ascent, as in the Gnostic-Hermetic-merkavah ascent of the soul), which are joined together in the ten sephiroth of kabbalah. There are five initiations, with further possibilities, and I found myself to be somewhat surprised that to be agreeing with his delineation of the stages involved in these, having myself been rather cynical as to any systematic definition of the stages of awakening. However, I do have a particular concern—and it is a fundamental one. Holman is very eclectic and I did find myself wondering time and again whether the writers on which he draws, and by extension Holam himself, though he makes no claim of spiritual advancement in the book, have actually experienced these initiations, personal deaths, openings and awakenings. The question is of course basic to following any spiritual system, teaching or teacher, but Holman's mode of writing is that of statement rather than speculation, and the word 'perhaps' might have been employed more frequently.

It is then quite a shock to jump to the final section of the book, with its emphasis on postmodernism, and the creation of a new spiritual psychology. Holman outlines the modern approaches of Jung, Roberto Assagioli and Ken Wilber, but rightly makes little attempt to integrate them into his earlier scheme. The overall impression of the book is of a strange blend of certainty and exploration. The book does a superb job of synthesising an intelkligent basic structure of western esotericism, but I am still left with the niggling question, 'where do we go from here?'

That said, each of these books is a genuinely useful guide to the western esoteric tradition. *The Golden Thread* is ideal as a first book. It is brief and insightful. So too is *Hidden Wisdom*, which gives fuller introductions to a wide variety of traditions, with excellent pointers to further study and practice. *The Return of the Perennial Philosophy* may be a little confusing for the absolute beginner, but contains plenty to discuss and chew over.

Andrew Phillip Smith

The Watkins Dictionary of Religious and Secular Faiths by Gerald Benedict. Watkins Publishing 708pp £12.99/$19.95

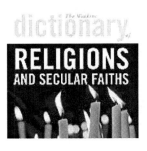

This is an extensive dictionary of medium-length entries. The slightly odd title means that secular responses to religious belief, and secular movements which may arguably be seen as a substitute for religious beliefs, political beliefs such as Marxism, scientific approaches such as Darwinism or secular philosophies such as humanism are also included. The secular entries are a clear minority and, opening the book at random, I had to turn 14 pages before I found a secular entry—in this case, entries for Nationalism and National Socialism. The dictionary would have been quite worthwhile without these, but it is nice to have articles on, for example, scientism or positivism in this context. As a dictionary of religion, it is thorough, and every subject that I looked up

had an entry. I also discovered much that I was unaware of, as for example a reformation protestant sect known as the Cokelers, who were founded in London in the mid-nineteenth century by a cobbler, and are found only in the counties of Sussex and Surrey. *The Watkins Dictionary of Religious and Secular Faiths* could occupy useful space on any reference shelf.

Andrew Phillip Smith

Gnosis! Sean Byrne, Age Old Press £8.99

Gnosis! is the first novel by Irish author Sean Byrne, blending fiction and non-fiction to create an intriguing look at the life of Origen, exploring early Christianity and Gnosticism, and giving a kind of 'inside look' into the world of the Second Century CE.

The book is published by Byrne's own small publishing company, Age Old Books. The quality of the print is good, as is the cover design (which depicts what looks like a rather bleak ancient metropolis), but there are some formatting issues. For a start, the borders are not an ideal size, and the chapter headings could do with some extra spacing before commencing into the text of the chapter itself; the way it is now leads it to look a little cluttered. Paragraphs are not indented, but spaced, and some clumps of dialogues are allotted a single paragraph, when it fact there should be one for each person's section of speech. The author also has a tendency to overuse the exclamation mark; it's not uncommon to see a number of instances on a single page. These things aren't the end of the world, least of all for a small print run by a small press, but they readily reveal themselves in comparison to the standards of bigger publishing houses, and may irritate the 'grammar nazis' among us. I had a hard time finding spelling errors or other notable grammar problems, however.

Now to the issues of the text itself. Obviously as a fictional novel we can't take what occurs in this book as historical fact, though it is definitely influenced by history (after all, Origen, among others the book centres on, was a historical figure). Exactly how much is fact and how much is fiction is a hard thing to weigh up, so unless you're already very familiar with the life of Origen and his writings, you may have a hard time telling this apart (and thus this is not a book to read as a biography of sorts). That aside, there are some other historical issues. In the Prologue Byrne states that Ancient Alexandria, particularly in the Second Century CE, 'was a time that is nowadays known to historians as The Gnosis'. I've never seen any historian or scholar ever refer to any period as 'The Gnosis', and I can't imagine why they would. Maybe 'the time of Gnosis' or something similar, but this seems to be a confusion between the genuine height of Gnosticism in this area and the Gnosis/Knowledge which they held so dear. As a Gnostic myself I have a hard time reconciling Byrne's use of 'Gnosis' as a kind of time period.

When you get into the text itself there are some good things and some bad things. Any familiar with the time period and figures mentioned will find it witty and intriguing (a good example is Origen's thoughts of other key figures of the time: 'Hippolytus did not know; Justin Martyr did not know; Iranaeus he simply could not stand…' Iranaeus frequently receives bad press among Gnostics [essentially returning the favour], so little tid-bits like this may make a Gnostic smile). The dialogue is interesting and accessible, and sometimes it reminds me of the style of the dialogue of Plato and Socrates (which is always good), though many modern phrases tend to creep in and jar the reality of the setting. There are issues, however, with point of view (the author switches between narrator and third-person frequently, which can be disconcerting). There is also a lot of telling of information and much less showing. I understand that Byrne needs to convey a fair amount of history, and back-story is always a tricky thing to work into a novel, but he usually pulls out of dialogue to impart an info-dump before swinging back into the dialogue again.

The book is fairly short (185) pages, and the chapters are quite short too, making it a much more digestible read. There's usually something of interest in each chapter, and while not everything is factual you'll frequently be exposed to nuggets of knowledge that may have thus far evaded you, as well as some good character development, particularly in Origen himself, who you cannot help but like more and more as you go through the story. Other strong characters include Clement, Ambrosius, Paul, and, of course, the matron Paula. You'll find plenty of entertainment in the interactions between these people.

Gnosis! is a fascinating look at the life of Origen with a fictional flare. If you want to know more about him without reaching for the dry academia, this is certainly the way to go. Indeed, there are few books like this, and that is definitely a reason alone to encourage more. However, don't take everything you read in this book as the truth – it simply won't replace a thorough biography or scholarly text. As a novel there are flaws, but it's Byrne's first novel, so that must be taken into consideration. However, none of these issues stop it from remaining a damn good read.

Dean Wilson

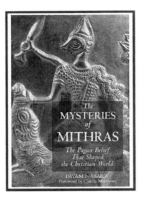

The Mysteries of Mithras; Payam Nabarz, Inner Traditions, 230pp, $14.95

On a brief visit to London last summer I found myself looking at a reconstructed Mithraeum—a cave-temple for the Mithraic religion—in the Museum of London. So it was with some interest that I came to review this book. The author, Payam Nabarz, is a neo-pagan, and the practice of a revived Mithraism is at the core of his approach, but he manages just the right blend of factual material and spiritual outlook. Despite the intrinsic anachronisms that must be involved in any revivalist approach (and Gnostic revivalism is no exception to this), I found myself warming to this book. Nabarz is careful to separate the Persian/Zoroastrian figure of Mithra from that of Mithras in the Mithraic religion proper, and his introductory chapters provide a good survey of Mithraism, drawing on many academic sources. Our textual knowledge of Mithraism is quite sketchy, but in the appendices Nabarz does include G.R.S. Mead's translation of the Mithraic Liturgy, plus two long Zoroastrian hymns related to Mithra.

Early chapters examine the iconography of Mithraism, which survives in the statuary and reliefs found in the Mithraic temples. Among the scenes depicted in the reliefs is the Mithraic sacred meal. Sacred meals are a feature common to many mystery religions among which may be included, according to some commentators (such as Helmut Koester), Christianity.

The seven initiatory levels of Mithraism, and the rites that accompany them, are the subject of an entire chapter. These are central to modern Mithraism, and many of the meditations and ceremonies given later in the book develop the outlines of these rites which survive in ancient sources. These may be of particular interest to Gnostics because of their relationship to the ascent of the soul.

A chapter is devoted to the Persian goddess Anahita, who is seen as bride and virginal mother of Mithras. Another to a Mithraic liturgy found in the Greek Magical Papyri. Here, Nabarz mingles the original text with guidelines for a reconstructed rite which may be practised.

The meditations, initiations and seasonal celebrations are given entirely from a neo-pagan point of view and, as I am not a neo-pagan and have no real connection with these forms, I can say little of their meaningfulness and efficacy, and so will pass over this section. A chapter-long treatment of the Persian Simorgh myth as a continuation of Mithraic influence was interesting, but I found myself unable to decide whether the story truly qualifies as Mithraic. The only section which seemed a little off to me is 'Echoes of Mithraism Around the World.' The similarities which the author claims to discover between Christian practice and Mithraism smack a little of parallelomania to me. Worse are the supposed parallels between Mithraism and Welsh and Irish myth—and I have a reasonable knowledge of the myths of the Celtic countries. Here the author relies on some very dubious sources and I found this chapter as a whole very unconvincing. The mix of Mithraism and neo-Celticism extends into the solstice and equinox celebrations which draw on modern pagan practices, and I should emphasise that I have no objection to syncretistism in itself, merely to dubious historical justifications.

Despite my initial dismay at the neo-pagan focus of this book, I found it to be a useful introduction, and for the most part the author successfully combines scholarship with a modern spiritual approach.

Andrew Phillip Smith

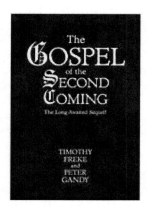

Gospel of the Second Coming, Tim Freke and Peter Gandy, Hay House, 208pp, £12.99/14.95

Few in the Gnostic and early Christian camp have been able to avoid Timothy Freke and Peter Gandy's controversial Jesus Trilogy—'The Jesus Mysteries', 'Jesus and the Lost Goddess' and 'The Laughing Jesus'. All three have expanded the dialog and interest in Gnosticism in the last decade. Although many have accused Freke and Gandy of bloating Gnosticism to any non-dualistic esoteric view, criticized them for playing theological total war against Orthodoxy, and uber-analyzed their daring scholarship, the Jesus Trilogy remains steadfast Solomonic pillars forever entrenched in the Gnostic revival.

So what is next when you've exhausted all forms of Gnostic worldviews—proto-Gnostic, Classic Gnostic and even Neo-Gnostic? 'Jesus vs. Mothra?' 'Jesus and Temple of Doom'? 'The Global Warming Jesus'. Simple. So simple we should all be doing it. Bishop Irenaeus of Lyons, the Lex Luthor of all Gnostics, complained in the late second century that Gnostics pumped out Gospels like Disney pumps out those awful straight to DVD sequels of classics.

So Freke and Gandy took a page from the Classic Gnostics and simply wrote their own evangelion, The Gospel of the Second Coming!!! The Gospel of the Second Coming is story within a story within a myth within another myth where Jesus understands he's just a fictional character. He teaches us that we are fictional characters as well, so wrapped up in our roles we won't just look up into the three-dimensionality of the Pleroma, the fullness of God, and comprehend that the cosmic joke is that we are also the authors of our own tragedies and victories. It seems so easy

when you think about it—recognize that you are a story-bound character and the plot no longer has any power over you. Exit stage left or just enjoy your role with both detached amusement and compassion for the other actors. Personally this was one of the few books I've read in a long time that made me laugh out loud. And that's a hard feat for the host of a show that gives serious glances at our failing civilization. But laugh I did like the Gnostic Jesus. And at the same time I was moved by the slapstick relationship of Jesus, Mary and Peter, the Gnostic tripartition of Spirit, Soul and Body.

The *Gospel of the Second Coming* accentuates these lines at the same time finding the solution to Peter, Simon and Mary's symbolic disagreement that has thundered throughout the last two thousand years. And it's Freke and Gandy's Jesus, a manifestation of their inner Christ that we all have as well, who finds a way to reconcile all the polarities after a wild Judgment Day at the climax of the story within a story and a myth within a another myth. This line encapsulates what you're in for when you read this modern gospel, 'The Gospel of the Second Coming will do to Christianity what Animal Farm did to Communism..

The *Gospel of the Second Coming* is also a recap of the Jesus Trilogy for those who haven't undergone the adventure, including Freke and Gandy's penchant of taking no prisoners. Yet it's all laid out in a humorous, odic and often bizarre tapestry, just like modern readers like to experience their websites or Xbox 360 games.

The Gospel of the Second Coming is moreover a book you can give to someone who seems to be struggling against their Fundamentalist tendencies but refuses to read esoteric scholarship to break the crazy glue of the Archons. Just like Richard Bach's *Jonathan Livingston Seagull* and *Illusions* pointed so many to the Eastern way of thinking, *The Gospel of the Second Coming* points to the Gnostic way of thinking… or more like being.!!! Worth the price, the read and whatever else makes Bishop Irenaeus irate.

Miguel Conner

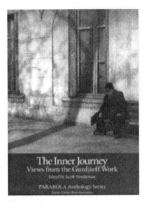

The Inner Journey: Views from the Gurdjieff Work; The Inner Journey: Myth, Psyche, and Spirit.

Parabola, a magazine of spirituality and mythology, has been published continuously for over thirty years. During this time a great number of fine articles by leading lights in a variety of subject areas have been amassed and *The Inner Journey series*, which now numbers eight volumes, has collected the best of these, organised by subject. 'Myth, Psyche and Spirit,' edited by Martha Heyneman, anthologises those contributions that cover the general subject of mythology, while 'Views from the Gurdjieff Work" focuses on the legacy of G.I. Gurdjieff, a subject close to the hearts of the magazine's editors. The contributions in the mythology volume range from translations and retellings of myths from many cultures to extracts from notable scholars such as Joseph Campbell, Mircea Eliade and Titus Burckhardt.

The Gurdjieff volume mixes extracts from Gurdjieff's own writings and his discourses as reported by others with articles by and interviews with his followers—mostly first-generation pupils of Gurdjieff associated with the 'official' Gurdjieff organisations, the Gurdjieff Foundation and its European equivalents. Topics include general discussions of the Gurdjieff work, Gurdjieff's music, methods of education, psychology and working in everyday life. Most of the contributors are unknown outside of work circles, but the filmmaker Peter Brook and Mary Poppins author Pamela Travers will be familiar to most readers.

These are weighty volumes that demand careful reading. The Gurdjieff volume is particularly good value as it includes a DVD of Peter Brook's film version of Gurdjieff's spiritual 'unreliable memoirs' *Meetings With Remarkable Men.* However, the film itself highlights a fundamental problem with *Parabola*. Peter Brook is a great director (his eight hour long Mahabharata is one of my favourite films.) Gurdjieff's original book provides extraordinary source material. Many of Gurdjieff's closest pupils, particularly Mme de Salzmann, were intimately involved with the making of the film, and Brook practises the Gurdjieff work himself. And yet the final result is over-respectful, flat, po-faced, and joyless. To a lesser extent this is true of Parabola. There is something a little over-refined about the articles. There are few laughs, little contention or controversy, and thus the end result lacks a certain sparkle or lightness of spirit. Perhaps the Gurdjieff volume could have been spiced with some of those bizarre anecdotes of the living Gurdjieff, or the volume on myth seasoned with the improper sexuality and danger of mythical stories. Yet, despite the lack of leaven, these volumes have a depth and breadth to them and are valuable collections.

Andrew Phillip Smith

The Gnostic Faustus: The Secret Teachings Behind the Classic Text, Romona Fradon, Inner Traditions, 384pp, £13.99/$19.95

The legend of Faust is a classic European model of the magus— Marlowe and Goethe made great literature out of it. A translation of the original Faust chapbook, the earliest surviving full version of the legend, is included, and it is rightly the basiis of Fradon's investigation. There are many resemblances between the story of the magician Faust and that of Simon Magus, which, with all its later elaborations, was well known in medieval and Renaissance Europe. The inclusion of a reference to Helen of Troy—who was a previous incarnation of Simon's love Helena and was Faust's magically summoned partner—in both is a particularly strong link between the two figures.

The main problem in Ramona Fradon's thesis is her insistence that the author of the Faust chapbook was aware of several texts in the Gnostic or Manichaean traditions, none of which were at all likely to be available in sixteenth century Europe either in Greek or Coptic or in Latin translation, which apart from the vernacular languages was the only language which they were likely to be able to read.

However, one could easily posit a genuinely historical connection between Faust and Manichaean ideas. Augustine's Contra Faustum, and other anti-Manichaean works of a much-admired Catholic church father, who wrote in Latin (sorry to labour the obvious points) would have been available and could be read by anyone with an education. There may be a case for the name deriving from Augustine's Manichaean opponent Faustus. Thus there is no need to claim unattested and exceptional survivals of Gnostic literature in order to argue a Gnostic or Manichaean influence on the Faust chapbook. But Augustine receives only a single mention.

Ramona Fradon proposes a massive mishmash of direct influences on the author of *Dr Faustus*: Tantric sexual practices, the *Apocryphon of John*, the *Exegesis on the Soul* and the *Tripartite Tractate*, Manichaean literature, John Dee's *Monas Hieroglyphica* and alchemy. It is only the last of these that is really feasible, or, in fact, probable, and here Ramona Fradon makes some nice suggestions for alchemical interpretation of the Faustus text. If you have a high tolerance for unlikely interpretations, then this book may be for you, but for anyone else,

the unreasonable hypothesis overwhelms and undermines the handful of genuinely insightful observations that Ramona Fradon's has to offer.

The idea that all of these could have influenced the author of Faustus is fairly ridiculous, but the line by line comparisons between the supposed source texts and Faustus would be parallelamania were there even any genuine parallels to be found—and most of Ramona Fradon's s parallels escape me. It would have been much better to have supposed an archetypal pattern that underlies both the Faust text and Gnostic texts without claiming any direct influence. Even this might have been problematic though, as Ramona Fradon's sees the Faust book as in many cases inverting the pattern.

Thus the book must, unfortunately, be considered a failure. Nevertheless, anyone who is really interested in the Faust legend and its esoteric implications, should go through the book with a critical toothcomb, sifting out the dross and gleaning the insights that could have been the foundation of a worthwhile book is a different approach had been taken.

Arthur Craddock

The Gnostics: History Tradition Scriptures Influence, Andrew Phillip Smith; Watkins Publishing, 248pp; £10.99; $14.95

THE GNOSTICS

ANDREW PHILLIP SMITH

HISTORY · TRADITION · SCRIPTURES · INFLUENCE ·

[Declaration of interest: the author of the book is editor of The Gnostic!] Gnosticism has become increasingly popular over recent years, with the publication of the Nag Hammadi library, the even more recent *Gospel of Judas*, the blockbuster *Matrix* films, and, of course, the infamous *Da Vinci Code* book and film, not to mention countless others that slip under the radar of all but those who have 'eyes to see'. However, all this popularity has led to a very skewed understanding of what Gnosticism is all about – some people think it was invented by Aleister Crowley, that it was all about Jesus' relationship with Mary Magdalene, or that it was a single obscure heretical group that didn't last very long. *The Gnostics*, by Andrew Phillip Smith, is an accessible book that dispels these erroneous views with a thorough introduction to the history, tradition, scriptures, and influence of Gnosticism in all its facets.

The book, numbering just under 250 pages, is broad in scope, dealing with nearly all of the Gnostic groups of note from its inception two millenia ago to its revival in modern days in both an occult and ecclesiastical form. Entire chapters are devoted to the Sethians and Valentinians, the Manichaens, the Cathars, and the Mandaens, with brief mention of other smaller groups (which we sadly lack information on) in between. Other chapters deal with Gnostic mythology, psychology, praxis, and, of course, that elusive concept of *Gnosis* itself. Smith includes a rather sizeable chapter on the modern Gnostic revival which 'brings it home', as it were, in a way that people can relate to; works from Blake, Philip Pullman, Philip K. Dick, and other modern works are mentioned, allowing the reader to see how the transmission of Gnosis never truly died out. References, a good bibliography, and an index are also supplied, which will please anyone looking at this from an academic perspective.

It is evident that Smith is not merely a scholar in this field, but immensely interested in the traditions and texts which he studies. His enthusiasm is apparent in nearly every page of the book, and his sympathy for Gnosticism is a welcome change for Gnostics like myself, who all too often have to contend with the cruel eye of heresiological bias. However, in stating this, Smith never abandons historical accuracy or conventional scholarly practice in presenting his views. His arguments are generally solid and widely accepted throughout the academic world. One such argument is 'Gnosticism is dualist', which frequently raises the ire of modern Gnostics who vehemently disagree with the notion. Initially a Gnostic reader might bite their lip when reading this same argument coming from Smith, but it quickly becomes apparent that he has found a balance between the conventional view and the modern Gnostic one: '...classical Gnostic dualism was a dualism within unity.' Smith also takes care not to lump every Gnostic group into the same 'dualistic' heading: 'There is a clear distinction between absolute or radical dualism [...] and mitigated or moderate dualism, which posits a good God or good force at the beginning and culmination, at the highest point of the universe, but which acknowledges that an independent evil force or lower God has as much, or more, influence on our present world. The Sethians and Valentinians were mitigated dualists, the Manichaens absolute dualists.' While many modern (Valentinian) Gnostics might still grind their teeth at the word 'dualist' being used here at all, this explict distinction between absolute and mitigated forms, so well described by Smith, goes a long way to amending the somewhat negative usage of the word.

The Gnostics is one of the few introductory texts that covers almost the entire scope of Gnosticism, providing a true and accurate portrayal of the variety and uniqueness that comes with Gnosis through the ages. In these days when people are questioning the orthodox Christian viewpoint, hungry now for a tradition that utilises the mythology they are used to in a radically different and positive way, it is important that they educate themselves on these alternate traditions that have remained a secret for too long in this world. In light of this, this book is one of the few I would recommend to those who know little or nothing about Gnosticism, and yet even for those who actively engage in the Gnostic path, for, as Smith puts it, 'the opportunities for Gnosis are greater now than they may have been for several centuries.'

Dean Wilson

Food for Thought

Every kind of mediation is alien to God.

Meister Eckhart

Gnosis should be an experience of your own life, a plant grown on your own tree. Foreign gods are a sweet poison, but the vegetable gods you have raised in your own garden are nourishing.

C.G. Jung, in a letter to Constance Long

The world is a bridge, so pass over it and do not inhabit it.

Jesus in the writings of Al Ghazali

As students of nature we are pantheists, as poets polytheists, as moral beings monotheists.

Goethe

For the important thing today is not so much to discover new stars as to break down the new frontiers that constantly arise before us, or which are delineated within ourselves, so that we may cross over them, as unto deat, with our eyes wide open.

Jacques Lacarrière

Principle I. That the Poetic Genius is the true Man, and that the body or outward form of Man is derived from the Poetic Genius. Likewise that the forms of all things are derived from their Genius, which by the Ancients was call'd an Angel & Spirit & Demon.

Principle II. As all men are alike in outward form, So (and with the same infinite variety) all are alike in the Poetic Genius.

William Blake, All Religions are One.

The beginning of perfection is the knowledge of Man, but the knowledge of God is complete perfection.

Naasenes.

There is a whole structure of teaching on this planet. It is like a strange other-dimensional house in which the rooms can act like 'keys' to other doors. Gurdjieff is a key to unlock the doors to certain rooms called 'Sufism', 'Gnosticism' and so on. These in their turn are keys to unlock the door marked 'Gurdjieff'.

Tony Blake

If 'nostalgia for the past' happens to coincide with nostalgia for the sacred, this is a virtue, not because it is directed to the past in itself, which would be quite devoid of meaning, but because it is directed towards the sacred, which transforms all duration into an eternal present and which cannot be situated elsewhere than in the liberating 'now' of God.

Frithjof Schuon

If a tyrant threatens you, especially at that time remember God.

Sentences of Sextus

Biographies

A.M. Ashford Brown is the author of many poems, collected in *Songs of Sorrow and Joy* and of an autobiographical novel, *Hedges, Ditches & Dreams*.

Arthur Craddock lives in the Welsh marches surrounded by sheep. His mammoth unpublished work, *The Grand Vision* takes a postmodern approach to spirituality that combines a powerful marketing ethic with what he calls 'arrogant esotericism'.

Eddie Campbell is the author of his autobiographical comics series *Alec* and illustrator of *From Hell*.

Miguel Conner is the author of the novel *Queen of Darkness* and host of the Internet radio show *Aeon Byte*, formerly *Coffee, Cigarettes and Gnosis*.

John Coulthart's designs and illustrations have appeared on record sleeves, CD and DVD packages for Cradle of Filth, Alan Moore & Tim Perkins, Steven Severin, Fourth World music pioneer Jon Hassell and many others. As a comic artist John produced the Lord Horror series 'Reverbstorm' with David Britton for Savoy Books. His collection of HP Lovecraft adaptations and illustrations, *The Haunter of the Dark and Other Grotesque Visions*, was republished in 2006 by Creation Oneiros.

Sven Davisson is the editor of *Ashé! Journal of Experimental Spirituality* (www.ashejournal. com) and publisher of Rebel Satori Press (www.rebelsatori.com). He is the author of the collection *The Starry Dynamo: The Machinery of Night Remixed*. In addition to *Ashé Journal*, his work has appeared in queer and occult magazines including *Abrasax: Journal of Magick & Decadence*, *sneerzine* and *Velvet Mafia*. His writing may also be found in the new collection *Madder Love: Queer Men and the Precincts of Surrealism*. Visit him at www.svendavisson.com

Scott Finch received his BFA from Louisiana State University in 1994 and his MFA from the Tyler School of Art at Temple University in 1996. Finch has exhibited at galleries across the United States and in Europe. He has been featured by the Critic's Choice Exhibition at the Dallas Visual Art Center, the Fleisher Art Challenge at the Fleisher Art Memorial in Philadelphia, and the Gulf South Regional Artists Exhibition at Bridge For Contemporary Art in New Orleans.

Jesse Folks is a graduate student earning a Masters in Coptic at Catholic University of America in Washington DC. He is trained in Greek and Coptic translation and New Testament text-criticism. He has been studying the Gnostic mythos for almost a decade. Jesse is also co-founder and administrator of the Palm Tree Garden, an online community for Gnostics and those interested in the study of Gnosticism.

Michael W. Grondin took an M.A. in Philosophy at Wayne State University, 1977 and is a specialist in Logic. He is self-taught in Sahidic Coptic and began study of the Coptic Gospel of Thomas in 1988. He is the creator of the first interlinear Coptic-English version of the Gospel ofIcthyas, hosted since 1996 on his website now called 'The Coptic Gospel of Thomas in Context' (http://www.geocities.com/Athens/9068/index.htm).

Alan Moore is the writer of *Voice of the Fire* and numerous comics and graphics novels including *Watchmen, V for Vendetta, From Hell, A Small Killing, Lost Girls, The League of Extraordinary Gentleman* and *Promethea,*

Will Parker is a writer and researcher, with a particular interest in the literature and history of Medieval Wales. His book, *The Four Branches of the Mabinogi*, was published by Bardic Press in 2005.

Andrew Phillip Smith is the editor of The Gnostic and author of *The Gnostics: History, Tradition, Scriptures, Influence, The Gospel of Philip: Annotated & Explained, The Lost Sayings of Jesus: Annotated & Explained,* and *Gnostic Writings on the Soul: Annotated & Explained.*

John D. Turner is both Professor of Religious Studies and Professor of Classics and History at the University of Nebraska-Lincoln. Professor Turner has devoted much of his academic career to Nag Hammadi studies both in terms of writing and service.

Luke Valentine is a practising Gnostic who lives in Jackson, Mississippi in the U.S. South where he writes and studies Gnostic scripture. He is an administrator of The Palm Tree Garden Gnostic web community and has a blog on the intersections of science and theology at http://infinitelyreal.blogspot.com. He is currently working on a chapter focusing on the Gnostic

life of Philip K. Dick for a collaborative book on contemporary Gnosticism.

Jim West is an independent theologian, researcher and mystic, and serves as the research staff writer for the Web forum *Coffee, Cigarettes and Gnosis*, hosted by Miguel Conner, a.k.a. Abraxas. Contact Jim at ogdood@yahoo.com.

Dean F. Wilson was born in Dublin, Ireland, where he currently resides. He's a practising Gnostic and ceremonial magician, and author of fiction and non fiction. More info can be found at: www.protosmythos.com

Also Available from Bardic Press

Boyhood With Gurdjieff; Gurdjieff Remembered; Balanced Man
by Fritz Peters (not available in the USA)

My Father Gurdjieff
Nicholas de Val

New Nightingale, New Rose: Poems From the Divan of Hafiz
translated by Richard Le Gallienne

The Quatrains of Omar Khayyam:
Three Translations of the Rubaiyat
*translated by Edward Fitzgerald, Justin McCarthy
and Richard Le Gallienne*

Door of the Bloved: Ghazals of Hafiz
translated by Justin McCarthy

The Gospel of Thomas and Christian Wisdom
Stevan Davies

The Four Branches of the Mabinogi
Will Parker

Christ In Islam
James Robson

Don't Forget: P.D. Ouspensly's Life of Self-Remembering
Bob Hunter

Songs of Sorrow and Joy
Ashford Brown

Planetary Types: The Science of Celestial Influence
Tony Cartledge

Visit our website at www.bardic-press.com
email us at info@bardic-press.com

LaVergne, TN USA
02 December 2010
206960LV00004B/151-160/P